THE WAR POEMS
of
SIEGFRIED SASSOON

Books by Siegfried Sassoon

MEMOIRS OF A FOX-HUNTING MAN
MEMOIRS OF AN INFANTRY OFFICER
SHERSTON'S PROGRESS
THE COMPLETE MEMOIRS OF GEORGE SHERSTON
THE OLD CENTURY
THE WEALD OF YOUTH
SIEGFRIED'S JOURNEY
COLLECTED POEMS
SELECTED POEMS

Edited by Rupert Hart-Davis

DIARIES 1915–1918
DIARIES 1920–1922

SIEGFRIED SASSOON

The War Poems

Arranged and introduced by
Rupert Hart-Davis

faber and faber

First published in 1983
by Faber and Faber Limited
3 Queen Square London WC1N 3AU
Set by Goodfellow & Egan Typesetters Ltd, Cambridge

Printed in England by
TJ International Ltd, Padstow, Cornwall

Poems © George Sassoon, 1983

Introduction and Notes © Rupert Hart-Davis, 1983

ISBN 0 571 13015 1
ISBN 978 0 571 13015 3

18 20 19

Contents

7

10

Introduction

In later years, when Siegfried Sassoon had written much else in prose and verse, he was annoyed at always being referred to simply as a war poet, but it was the Great War that turned him into a poet of international fame, and I feel sure that his ghost will forgive me for thus bringing together these magnificently scarifying poems.

I have arranged them as far as possible in the order of their composition, and the reader can compare them with the poet's movements by means of the Biographical Table on pp.13–14.

Of these 113 poems, ninety-three come from Sassoon's published books, seven from periodicals and thirteen from manuscripts. Thirty-three of them can, on the poet's authority (from his diary and other notes), be attributed to exact days. On the same authority, and from other sources, many more can be placed in a month. The poems noted simply as written at Craiglockhart can be dated only between July and December 1917.

There is ample evidence to show that usually a finished poem which the poet thought good enough was almost immediately sent to a periodical and published there within a few days. I have printed the dates of such publications as at least a rough guide to the time of composition. For the dates of the first publication of the other poems readers should refer to Sir Geoffrey Keynes's bibliography, which has been an immense help to me.

Of the remaining poems, of which no periodical publication is known, I can give only the dates on which they appeared in *Counter-Attack* (1918) or *War Poems* (1919).

The notes that follow some of the poems are the poet's; the ones at the foot of the page are mine. All the texts are taken from manuscripts or from the last printed version. Few of them underwent more than minor alteration at any stage.

I am most grateful to Kenneth A. Lohf of New York for sending

11

me a photocopy of the manuscript of 'A Footnote on the War', and to Jon Silkin for the same kindness with regard to 'A Night Attack'.

Marske-in-Swaledale   RUPERT HART-DAVIS
October 1982

Biographical Table

1886	September 8	Siegfried Sassoon born at Weirleigh, near Paddock Wood, in Kent.
1914	August 3	Enlisted as trooper in Sussex Yeomanry.
1915	May	Commissioned in Royal Welch Fusiliers.
	November 24	Joined First Battalion RWF in France.
1916	April 20	To Fourth Army School at Flixécourt for four-week course.
	June	Awarded Military Cross for gallantry in action.
	August 2	Invalided home with trench fever. In hospital at Somerville College, Oxford. Convalescent at Weirleigh.
	December 4	Reported to Regimental Depot at Litherland, near Liverpool.
1917	February 16	Arrived at Infantry Base Depot, Rouen.
	February 18–27	In 25 Stationary Hospital, Rouen, with German measles.
	March 11	Joined Second Battalion RWF on the Somme front.
	April 16	Wounded in shoulder.
	April 20	In hospital at Denmark Hill.
	May 8	*The Old Huntsman* published.
	May 12–June 4	In convalescent home at Chapelwood Manor, Nutley, Sussex.
	July 20	Attended Medical Board at Liverpool. Sent to Craiglockhart War Hospital, near Edinburgh, where he was a patient of W.H.R. Rivers and met Wilfred Owen.
	July 30	His statement against the continuation of the war read out in House of Commons and reported in *The Times* next day.
	November 26	Passed fit for General Service.

	December 11	Reported back to Litherland.
1918	January 7	Posted to Limerick.
	February 8	Posted to Palestine with Twenty-Fifth Battalion R. W. F.
	May 9	Battalion arrived in France.
	June 27	*Counter-Attack* published.
	July 13	Wounded in head. To American Red Cross Hospital, 98 Lancaster Gate.
	August 20	To convalescent home at Lennel House, near Coldstream in Berwickshire. Thereafter on indefinite sick-leave.
1919	March 12	Officially retired from Army.
	October 30	*War Poems* published.

Absolution

The anguish of the earth absolves our eyes
Till beauty shines in all that we can see.
War is our scourge; yet war has made us wise,
And, fighting for our freedom, we are free.

Horror of wounds and anger at the foe,
And loss of things desired; all these must pass.
We are the happy legion, for we know
Time's but a golden wind that shakes the grass.

There was an hour when we were loth to part
From life we longed to share no less than others.
Now, having claimed this heritage of heart,
What need we more, my comrades and my brothers?

April–September 1915

People used to feel like this when they 'joined up' in 1914 and 1915. No one feels it when they 'go out again'. They only feel, then, a queer craving for 'good old times at Givenchy' etc. But there will always be 'good old times', even for people promoted from Inferno to Paradise!

The Redeemer

Darkness: the rain sluiced down; the mire was deep;
It was past twelve on a mid-winter night,
When peaceful folk in beds lay snug asleep;
There, with much work to do before the light,
We lugged our clay-sucked boots as best we might
Along the trench; sometimes a bullet sang,
And droning shells burst with a hollow bang;
We were soaked, chilled and wretched, every one;
Darkness; the distant wink of a huge gun.

I turned in the black ditch, loathing the storm;
A rocket fizzed and burned with blanching flare,
And lit the face of what had been a form
Floundering in mirk. He stood before me there;
I say that He was Christ; stiff in the glare;
And leaning forward from His burdening task,
Both arms supporting it; His eyes on mine
Stared from the woeful head that seemed a mask
Of mortal pain in Hell's unholy shine.

No thorny crown, only a woollen cap
He wore—an English soldier, white and strong,
Who loved his time like any simple chap,
Good days of work and sport and homely song;
Now he has learned that nights are very long,
And dawn a watching of the windowed sky.
But to the end, unjudging, he'll endure
Horror and pain, not uncontent to die
That Lancaster on Lune may stand secure.

He faced me, reeling in his weariness,
Shouldering his load of planks, so hard to bear.
I say that He was Christ, who wrought to bless
All groping things with freedom bright as air,
And with His mercy washed and made them fair.
Then the flame sank, and all grew black as pitch,
While we began to struggle along the ditch;
And someone flung his burden in the muck,
Mumbling: "O Christ Almighty, now I'm stuck!"

November 1915/March 1916

My first front-line poem. Written November 1915, inspired by
working-parties at Festubert, Nov. 25 and 27. (I joined the First
Battalion on Nov. 24.) Revised and rewritten March 1916. Steel hats
weren't the fashion until the spring of 1916 —hence the 'woollen cap'.

17

To My Brother

Give me your hand, my brother, search my face;
Look in these eyes lest I should think of shame;
For we have made an end of all things base.
We are returning by the road we came.

Your lot is with the ghosts of soldiers dead,
And I am in the field where men must fight.
But in the gloom I see your laurell'd head
And through your victory I shall win the light.

18 December 1915

Originally titled 'Brothers'. S.S.'s younger brother Hamo had been
buried at sea on 1 November 1915 after being mortally wounded at
Gallipoli. He was twenty-eight.

The Prince of Wounds

The Prince of wounds is with us here;
Wearing his crown he gazes down,
Sad and forgiving and austere.
We have renounced our lovely things,
Music and colour and delight:
The spirit of Destruction sings
And tramples on the flaring night.
But Christ is here upon the cross,
Bound to a road that's dark with blood,
Guarding immitigable loss.
Have we the strength to strive alone
Who can no longer worship Christ?
Is He a God of wood and stone,
While those who served him writhe and moan,
On warfare's altar sacrificed?

27 December 1915

Text from manuscript.

A Testament

If, as I think, I'm warned to pack and go
On a longer journey than I've made before,
I must be taking stock of what I leave,
And what I stand to lose, of all my store,

Cries for completion. Things, that made me weep
For joy of loveliness, come shining back
Dazzling my spirit that prepares for sleep.

Hushed is the house that once was full of songs.
In stillness rich with music that has been,
I wait death's savage hour that shall deliver
My soul and leave the soaring night serene.

There was a narrow path from glade to glade
Threading the golden forest, like a story
Planned to no certain close; a path that went
From morning to a sundown spilt with glory:

My home was safe among the slender trees;
There, on the blossomed slopes of time and sense,
Birds flocked and days came delicate and cold;
But now the tempest stoops to bear me hence.

The arches of the air are mighty songs
That tell me of a wide-flung radiance spread
Across the world; my feet roam with the tides,
And I am crowned with the triumphant dead.

Montagne, 1 January 1916

Text from manuscript.

To Victory

(TO EDMUND GOSSE)

Return to greet me, colours that were my joy,
Not in the woeful crimson of men slain,
But shining as a garden; come with the streaming
Banners of dawn and sundown after rain.

I want to fill my gaze with blue and silver,
Radiance through living roses, spires of green
Rising in young-limbed copse and lovely wood
Where the hueless wind passes and cries unseen.

I am not sad; only I long for lustre.
I am tired of the greys and browns and the leafless ash.
I would have hours that move like a glitter of dancers
Far from the angry guns that boom and flash.

Return, musical, gay with blossom and fleetness,
Days when my sight shall be clear and my heart rejoice;
Come from the sea with breadth of approaching brightness,
When the blithe wind laughs on the hills with uplifted voice.

4 January 1916

Printed anonymously in *The Times* on 15 January.

21

In the Pink

So Davies wrote: "This leaves me in the pink."
Then scrawled his name: "Your loving sweetheart, Willie."
With crosses for a hug. He'd had a drink
Of rum and tea; and, though the barn was chilly,
For once his blood ran warm; he had pay to spend.
Winter was passing; soon the year would mend.

But he couldn't sleep that night; stiff in the dark
He groaned and thought of Sundays at the farm,
And how he'd go as cheerful as a lark
In his best suit, to wander arm in arm
With brown-eyed Gwen, and whisper in her ear
The simple, silly things she liked to hear.

And then he thought: to-morrow night we trudge
Up to the trenches, and my boots are rotten.
Five miles of stodgy clay and freezing sludge,
And everything but wretchedness forgotten.
To-night he's in the pink; but soon he'll die.
And still the war goes on——*he* don't know why.

10 February 1916

The first of my 'outspoken' war poems. I wrote it one cold morning at
Morlancourt, sitting by the fire in the Quartermaster's billet, while our
Machine-Gun Officer shivered in his blankets on the floor. He was
suffering from alcoholic poisoning, and cold feet, and shortly afterwards
departed for England, never to return. Needless to say, the verses do not
refer to him, but to some typical Welshman who probably got killed on
the Somme in July, after months and months of a dog's life and no leave.
The *Westminster* refused the poem, as they thought it might prejudice
recruiting!!

22

The Dragon and the Undying

All night the flares go up; the Dragon sings
And beats upon the dark with furious wings;
And, stung to rage by his own darting fires,
Reaches with grappling coils from town to town;
He lusts to break the loveliness of spires,
And hurl their martyred music toppling down.

Yet, though the slain are homeless as the breeze,
Vocal are they, like storm-bewilder'd seas.
Their faces are the fair, unshrouded night,
And planets are their eyes, their ageless dreams.
Tenderly stooping earthward from their height,
They wander in the dusk with chanting streams,
And they are dawn-lit trees, with arms up-flung,
To hail the burning heavens they left unsung.

February 1916

Golgotha

Through darkness curves a spume of falling flares
That flood the field with shallow, blanching light.
   The huddled sentry stares
   On gloom at war with white,
   And white receding slow, submerged in gloom.
   Guns into mimic thunder burst and boom,
   And mirthless laughter rakes the whistling night.
The sentry keeps his watch where no one stirs
But the brown rats, the nimble scavengers.

March 1916

Written in trenches. The weather beastly wet and the place was like the end of the world.

24

A Subaltern

He turned to me with his kind, sleepy gaze
And fresh face slowly brightening to the grin
That sets my memory back to summer days,
With twenty runs to make, and last man in.
He told me he'd been having a bloody time
In trenches, crouching for the crumps to burst,
While squeaking rats scampered across the slime
And the grey palsied weather did its worst.
But as he stamped and shivered in the rain,
My stale philosophies had served him well;
Dreaming about his girl had sent his brain
Blanker than ever—she'd no place in Hell . . . .
"Good God!" he laughed, and slowly filled his pipe,
Wondering "why he always talks such tripe".

March 1916

D. C. Thomas, killed on March 18. I wrote this about ten days before,
when he'd been telling me how my sage advice had helped him along.
He appears again the 'The Last Meeting' and 'A Letter Home'.

A Working Party

Three hours ago he blundered up the trench,
Sliding and poising, groping with his boots;
Sometimes he tripped and lurched against the walls
With hands that pawed the sodden bags of chalk.
He couldn't see the man who walked in front;
Only he heard the drum and rattle of feet
Stepping along barred trench-boards, often splashing
Wretchedly where the sludge was ankle-deep.

Voices would grunt "Keep to your right—make way!"
When squeezing past some men from the front line:
White faces peered, puffing a point of red;
Candles and braziers glinted through the chinks
And curtain-flaps of dug-outs; then the gloom
Swallowed his sense of sight; he stopped and swore
Because a sagging wire had caught his neck.

A flare went up; the shining whiteness spread
And flickered upward, showing nimble rats
And mounds of glimmering sandbags, bleached with rain;
Then the slow silver moment died in dark.
The wind came posting by with chilly gusts
And buffeting at corners, piping thin
And dreary through the crannies; rifle-shots
Would split and crack and sing along the night,
And shells came calmly through the drizzling air
To burst with hollow bang below the hill.

Three hours ago he stumbled up the trench;
Now he will never walk that road again:
He must be carried back, a jolting lump
Beyond all need of tenderness and care.

He was a young man with a meagre wife
And two small children in a Midland town;
He showed their photographs to all his mates,
And they considered him a decent chap
Who did his work and hadn't much to say,
And always laughed at other people's jokes
Because he hadn't any of his own.

That night when he was busy at his job
Of piling bags along the parapet,
He thought how slow time went, stamping his feet
And blowing on his fingers, pinched with cold.
He thought of getting back by half-past twelve,
And tot of rum to send him warm to sleep
In draughty dug-out frowsty with the fumes
Of coke, and full of snoring weary men.

He pushed another bag along the top,
Craning his body outward; then a flare
Gave one white glimpse of No Man's Land and wire;
And as he dropped his head the instant split
His startled life with lead, and all went out.

30 March 1916

Written while in the Front Line during my first tour of trenches.

27

Stand-to: Good Friday Morning

I'd been on duty from two till four.
I went and stared at the dug-out door.
Down in the frowst I heard them snore.
"Stand to!" Somebody grunted and swore.
 Dawn was misty; the skies were still;
 Larks were singing, discordant, shrill;
 They seemed happy; but *I* felt ill.
Deep in water I splashed my way
Up the trench to our bogged front line.
Rain had fallen the whole damned night.
O Jesus, send me a wound to-day,
And I'll believe in Your bread and wine,
And get my bloody old sins washed white!

22 April 1916

I haven't shown this to any clergyman. But soldiers say they feel like that sometimes. So the parsons must turn over two pages at once and pray for all poor heretics.

The Kiss

To these I turn, in these I trust—
Brother Lead and Sister Steel.
To his blind power I make appeal,
I guard her beauty clean from rust.

He spins and burns and loves the air,
And splits a skull to win my praise;
But up the nobly marching days
She glitters naked, cold and fair.

Sweet Sister, grant your soldier this:
That in good fury he may feel
The body where he sets his heel
Quail from your downward darting kiss.

Flixécourt, 25 April 1916

A famous Scotch Major (Campbell) came and lectured on the bayonet.
'The bayonet and the bullet are brother and sister,' he said.

France

She triumphs, in the vivid green
Where sun and quivering foliage meet;
And in each soldier's heart serene;
When death stood near them they have seen
The radiant forests where her feet
Move on a breeze of silver sheen.

And they are fortunate, who fight
For gleaming landscapes swept and shafted
And crowned by cloud pavilions white;
Hearing such harmonies as might
Only from Heaven be downward wafted—
Voices of victory and delight.

Flixécourt, May 1916

The Last Meeting

I

Because the night was falling warm and still
Upon a golden day at April's end,
I thought; I will go up the hill once more
To find the face of him that I have lost,[1]
And speak with him before his ghost has flown
Far from the earth that might not keep him long.

So down the road I went, pausing to see
How slow the dusk drew on, and how the folk
Loitered about their doorways, well-content
With the fine weather and the waxing year.
The miller's house, that glimmered with grey walls,
Turned me aside; and for a while I leaned
Along the tottering rail beside the bridge
To watch the dripping mill-wheel green with damp.
The miller peered at me with shadowed eyes
And pallid face: I could not hear his voice
For sound of the weir's plunging. He was old.
His days went round with the unhurrying wheel.

Moving along the street, each side I saw
The humble, kindly folk in lamp-lit rooms;
Children at table; simple, homely wives;
Strong, grizzled men; and soldiers back from war,
Scaring the gaping elders with loud talk.

Soon all the jumbled roofs were down the hill,
And I was turning up the grassy lane
That goes to the big, empty house that stands

See note, p. 25.

Above the town, half-hid by towering trees.
I looked below and saw the glinting lights:
I heard the treble cries of bustling life,
And mirth, and scolding; and the grind of wheels.
An engine whistled, piercing-shrill, and called
High echoes from the sombre slopes afar;
Then a long line of trucks began to move.

It was quite still; the columned chestnuts stood
Dark in their noble canopies of leaves.
I thought: "A little longer I'll delay,
And then he'll be more glad to hear my feet,
And with low laughter ask me why I'm late.
The place will be too dim to show his eyes,
But he will loom above me like a tree,
With lifted arms and body tall and strong."

There stood the empty house; a ghostly hulk
Becalmed and huge, massed in the mantling dark,
As builders left it when quick-shattering war
Leapt upon France and called her men to fight.
Lightly along the terraces I trod,
Crunching the rubble till I found the door
That gaped in twilight, framing inward gloom.
An owl flew out from under the high eaves
To vanish secretly among the firs,
Where lofty boughs netted the gleam of stars.
I stumbled in; the dusty floors were strewn
With cumbering piles of planks and props and beams;
Tall windows gapped the walls; the place was free
To every searching gust and jousting gale;
But now they slept; I was afraid to speak,
And heavily the shadows crowded in.

I called him, once; then listened: nothing moved:
Only my thumping heart beat out the time.
Whispering his name, I groped from room to room.

Quite empty was that house; it could not hold
His human ghost, remembered in the love
That strove in vain to be companioned still.

II

Blindly I sought the woods that I had known
So beautiful with morning when I came
Amazed with spring that wove the hazel twigs
With misty raiment of awakening green.
I found a holy dimness, and the peace
Of sanctuary, austerely built of trees,
And wonder stooping from the tranquil sky.

Ah! but there was no need to call his name.
He was beside me now, as swift as light.
I knew him crushed to earth in scentless flowers,
And lifted in the rapture of dark pines.
"For now," he said, "my spirit has more eyes
Than heaven has stars; and they are lit by love.
My body is the magic of the world,
And dawn and sunset flame with my spilt blood.
My breath is the great wind, and I am filled
With molten power and surge of the bright waves
That chant my doom along the ocean's edge.

"Look in the faces of the flowers and find
The innocence that shrives me; stoop to the stream
That you may share the wisdom of my peace.
For talking water travels undismayed.

The luminous willows lean to it with tales
Of the young earth; and swallows dip their wings
Where showering hawthorn strews the lanes of light.

"I can remember summer in one thought
Of wind-swept green, and deeps of melting blue,
And scent of limes in bloom; and I can hear
Distinct the early mower in the grass,
Whetting his blade along some morn of June.

"For I was born to the round world's delight,
And knowledge of enfolding motherhood,
Whose tenderness, that shines through constant toil,
Gathers the naked children to her knees.
In death I can remember how she came
To kiss me while I slept; still I can share
The glee of childhood; and the fleeting gloom
When all my flowers were washed with rain of tears.

"I triumph in the choruses of birds,
Bursting like April buds in gyres of song.
My meditations are the blaze of noon
On silent woods, where glory burns the leaves.
I have shared breathless vigils; I have slaked
The thirst of my desires in bounteous rain
Pouring and splashing downward through the dark.
Loud storm has roused me with its winking glare,
And voice of doom that crackles overhead.
I have been tired and watchful, craving rest,
Till the slow-footed hours have touched my brows
And laid me on the breast of sundering sleep."

III

I know that he is lost among the stars,
And may return no more but in their light.
Though his hushed voice may call me in the stir
Of whispering trees, I shall not understand.
Men may not speak with stillness; and the joy
Of brooks that leap and tumble down green hills
Is faster than their feet; and all their thoughts
Can win no meaning from the talk of birds.

My heart is fooled with fancies, being wise;
For fancy is the gleaming of wet flowers
When the hid sun looks forth with golden stare.
Thus, when I find new loveliness to praise,
And things long-known shine out in sudden grace,
Then will I think: "He moves before me now."
So he will never come but in delight,
And, as it was in life, his name shall be
Wonder awaking in a summer dawn,
And youth, that dying, touched my lips to song.

Flixécourt, May 1916

A Letter Home

(TO ROBERT GRAVES)

I

Here I'm sitting in the gloom
Of my quiet attic room.
France goes rolling all around,
Fledged with forest May has crowned.
And I puff my pipe, calm-hearted,
Thinking how the fighting started,
Wondering when we'll ever end it,
Back to Hell with Kaiser send it,
Gag the noise, pack up and go,
Clockwork soldiers in a row.
I've got better things to do
Than to waste my time on you.

II

Robert, when I drowse to-night,
Skirting lawns of sleep to chase
Shifting dreams in mazy light,
Somewhere then I'll see your face
Turning back to bid me follow
Where I wag my arms and hollo,
Over hedges hasting after
Crooked smile and baffling laughter.
  Running tireless, floating, leaping,
  Down your web-hung woods and valleys,
  Garden glooms and hornbeam alleys,
  Where the glowworm stars are peeping,
  Till I find you, quiet as stone
  On a hill-top all alone,
  Staring outward, gravely pondering
  Jumbled leagues of hillock-wandering.

36

III

You and I have walked together
In the starving winter weather.
We've been glad because we knew
Time's too short and friends are few.
We've been sad because we missed
One whose yellow head was kissed
By the gods, who thought about him
Till they couldn't do without him.
Now he's here again; I've seen
Soldier David dressed in green,
Standing in a wood that swings
To the madrigal he sings.
He's come back, all mirth and glory,
Like the prince in fairy story.
Winter called him far away;
Blossoms bring him home with May.

IV

Well, I know you'll swear it's true
That you found him decked in blue
Striding up through morning-land
With a cloud on either hand.
Out in Wales, you'll say, he marches,
Arm in arm with oaks and larches;
Hides all night in hilly nooks,
Laughs at dawn in tumbling brooks.
   Yet, it's certain, here he teaches
   Outpost-schemes to groups of beeches.
   And I'm sure, as here I stand,
   That he shines through every land,
   That he sings in every place
   Where we're thinking of his face.

V

Robert, there's a war in France;
Everywhere men bang and blunder,
Sweat and swear and worship Chance,
Creep and blink through cannon thunder.
Rifles crack and bullets flick,
Sing and hum like hornet-swarms.
Bones are smashed and buried quick.
    Yet, through stunning battle storms,
    All the while I watch the spark
    Lit to guide me; for I know
    Dreams will triumph, though the dark
    Scowls above me where I go.
You can hear me; you can mingle
Radiant folly with my jingle.
War's a joke for me and you
While we know such dreams are true!

Flixécourt, May 1916

Graves replied with a verse letter, published in his *Fairies and Fusiliers*
(1917) as 'Letter to S.S. from Mametz Wood'. For David, see note,
p. 25.

Before the Battle

Music of whispering trees
Hushed by a broad-winged breeze
Where shaken water gleams;
And evening radiance falling
With reedy bird-notes calling.
O bear me safe through dark, you low-voiced streams.

I have no need to pray
That fear may pass away;
I scorn the growl and rumble of the fight
That summons me from cool
Silence of marsh and pool
And yellow lilies islanded in light.
O river of stars and shadows, lead me through the night.

Bussy-le-Daours, 25 June 1916

The Battle of the Somme began on 1 July.

At Carnoy

Down in the hollow there's the whole Brigade
Camped in four groups: through twilight falling slow
I hear a sound of mouth-organs, ill-played,
And murmur of voices, gruff, confused, and low.
Crouched among thistle-tufts I've watched the glow
Of a blurred orange sunset flare and fade;
And I'm content. To-morrow we must go
To take some cursèd Wood. . . . O world God made!

3 July 1916

Died of Wounds

His wet white face and miserable eyes
Brought nurses to him more than groans and sighs:
But hoarse and low and rapid rose and fell
His troubled voice: he did the business well.

The ward grew dark; but he was still complaining
And calling out for "Dickie". "Curse the Wood!
It's time to go. O Christ, and what's the good?
We'll never take it, and it's always raining."

I wondered where he'd been; then heard him shout,
"They snipe like hell! O Dickie, don't go out" . . . .
I fell asleep. . . . Next morning he was dead;
And some Slight Wound lay smiling on the bed.

July 1916

I got the idea in the hospital at Amiens, where a youngster raved and
died in the bed opposite mine. I think he came from High Wood at its
worst.

A Night Attack

The rank stench of those bodies haunts me still,
And I remember things I'd best forget.
For now we've marched to a green, trenchless land
Twelve miles from battering guns: along the grass
Brown lines of tents are hives for snoring men;
Wide, radiant water sways the floating sky
Below dark, shivering trees. And living-clean
Comes back with thoughts of home and hours of sleep.

To-night I smell the battle; miles away
Gun-thunder leaps and thuds along the ridge;
The spouting shells dig pits in fields of death,
And wounded men are moaning in the woods.
If any friend be there whom I have loved,
God speed him safe to England with a gash.

It's sundown in the camp; some youngster laughs,
Lifting his mug and drinking health to all
Who come unscathed from that unpitying waste.
(Terror and ruin lurk behind his gaze.)
Another sits with tranquil, musing face,
Puffing his pipe and dreaming of the girl
Whose last scrawled letter lies upon his knee.
The sunlight falls, low-ruddy from the west,
Upon their heads; last week they might have died;
And now they stretch their limbs in tired content.

One says "The bloody Bosche has got the knock;
And soon they'll crumple up and chuck their games.
We've got the beggars on the run at last!"
    Then I remembered someone that I'd seen
Dead in a squalid, miserable ditch,
Heedless of toiling feet that trod him down.

He was a Prussian with a decent face,
Young, fresh, and pleasant, so I dare to say.
No doubt he loathed the war and longed for peace,
And cursed our souls because we'd killed his friends.

One night he yawned along a half-dug trench
Midnight; and then the British guns began
With heavy shrapnel bursting low, and "hows"
Whistling to cut the wire with blinding din.
    He didn't move; the digging still went on;
Men stooped and shovelled; someone gave a grunt,
And moaned and died with agony in the sludge.
Then the long hiss of shells lifted and stopped.

He stared into the gloom; a rocket curved,
And rifles rattled angrily on the left
Down by the wood, and there was noise of bombs.
    Then the damned English loomed in scrambling haste
Out of the dark and struggled through the wire,
And there were shouts and curses; someone screamed
And men began to blunder down the trench
Without their rifles. It was time to go:
He grabbed his coat; stood up, gulping some bread;
Then clutched his head and fell.
                                        I found him there
In the gray morning when the place was held.
His face was in the mud; one arm flung out
As when he crumpled up; his sturdy legs
Were bent beneath his trunk; heels to the sky.

July 1916

Published only in *Stand*, vol. 12, no. 1, 1970–1. Text from manuscript.

To His Dead Body

When roaring gloom surged inward and you cried,
Groping for friendly hands, and clutched, and died,
Like racing smoke, swift from your lolling head
Phantoms of thought and memory thinned and fled.

Yet, though my dreams that throng the darkened stair
Can bring me no report of how you fare,
Safe quit of wars, I speed you on your way
Up lonely, glimmering fields to find new day,
Slow-rising, saintless, confident and kind—
Dear, red-faced father God who lit your mind.

July 1916

Written in hospital at Amiens at the end of July 1916. It refers to Robert Graves, who had been reported Died of Wounds. A fortnight later Eddie Marsh wired to me at Oxford that R.G. was doing well and in hospital at Highgate.

Christ and the Soldier

I

The straggled soldier halted—stared at Him—
Then clumsily dumped down upon his knees,
Gasping, "O blessed crucifix, I'm beat!"
And Christ, still sentried by the seraphim,
Near the front-line, between two splintered trees,
Spoke him: "My son, behold these hands and feet."

The soldier eyed Him upward, limb by limb,
Paused at the Face; then muttered, "Wounds like these
Would shift a bloke to Blighty just a treat!"
Christ, gazing downward, grieving and ungrim,
Whispered, "I made for you the mysteries,
Beyond all battles moves the Paraclete."

II

The soldier chucked his rifle in the dust,
And slipped his pack, and wiped his neck, and said—
"O Christ Almighty, stop this bleeding fight!"
Above that hill the sky was stained like rust
With smoke. In sullen daybreak flaring red
The guns were thundering bombardment's blight.

The soldier cried, "I was born full of lust,
With hunger, thirst, and wishfulness to wed.
Who cares today if I done wrong or right?"
Christ asked all pitying, "Can you put no trust
In my known word that shrives each faithful head?
Am I not resurrection, life and light?"

III

Machine-guns rattled from below the hill;
High bullets flicked and whistled through the leaves;
And smoke came drifting from exploding shells.
Christ said, "Believe; and I can cleanse your ill.
I have not died in vain between two thieves;
Nor made a fruitless gift of miracles."

The soldier answered, "Heal me if you will,
Maybe there's comfort when a soul believes
In mercy, and we need it in these hells.
But be you for both sides? I'm paid to kill
And if I shoot a man his mother grieves.
Does that come into what your teaching tells?"

A bird lit on the Christ and twittered gay;
Then a breeze passed and shook the ripening corn.
A Red Cross waggon bumped along the track.
Forsaken Jesus dreamed in the desolate day—
Uplifted Jesus, Prince of Peace forsworn—
An observation post for the attack.

"Lord Jesus, ain't you got no more to say?"
Bowed hung that head below the crown of thorns.
The soldier shifted, and picked up his pack,
And slung his gun, and stumbled on his way.
"O God," he groaned, "why ever was I born?" . . .
The battle boomed, and no reply came back.

5 August 1916

Written at Somerville College, Oxford. I never showed this to anyone,
realizing that it was an ambitious failure. I intended it to be a

commentary on the mental condition of most front-line soldiers, for whom a roadside Calvary was merely a reminder of the inability of religion to co-operate with the carnage and catastrophe they experienced.

The dilemma of an ignorant private is demonstrated. But I was a very incomplete and quite unpractising Christian, and understood little more than he of the meaning of Our Lord's teaching. Like Wilfred Owen, I was anti-clerical, and the Churches seemed to offer no solution to the demented doings on the Western Front. My carefully contrived attempt at a potent parable certainly wasn't worth printing. Could *anyone*—from a fully informed religious understanding—have made a success of the subject?

As far as I can remember, no one at the Front ever talked to me about religion at all. And the padrés never came near us—except to bury someone. (An exception was Maurice Peel, who was killed with our First Battalion at Bullecourt in April 1917—a byword for bravery.)

This poem cannot be read as showing any clue to my own mental position, which was altogether confused, and became increasingly disillusioned and rebellious. (I wrote 'They' three months afterwards.) Like the soldier in the poem, all I could say was 'O Jesus, make it stop!'

Published only in *Siegfried Sassoon: Poet's Pilgrimage*, assembled by Dame Felicitas Corrigan (1973). Text from manuscript.

The One-Legged Man

Propped on a stick he viewed the August weald;
Squat orchard trees and oasts with painted cowls;
A homely, tangled hedge, a corn-stalked field,
And sound of barking dogs and farmyard fowls.

And he'd come home again to find it more
Desirable than ever it was before.
How right it seemed that he should reach the span
Of comfortable years allowed to man!

Splendid to eat and sleep and choose a wife,
Safe with his wound, a citizen of life.
He hobbled blithely through the garden gate,
And thought: "Thank God they had to amputate!"

August 1916

The Hero

"Jack fell as he'd have wished," the Mother said,
And folded up the letter that she'd read.
"The Colonel writes so nicely." Something broke
In the tired voice that quavered to a choke.
She half looked up. "We mothers are so proud
Of our dead soldiers." Then her face was bowed.

Quietly the Brother Officer went out.
He'd told the poor old dear some gallant lies
That she would nourish all her days, no doubt.
For while he coughed and mumbled, her weak eyes
Had shone with gentle triumph, brimmed with joy,
Because he'd been so brave, her glorious boy.

He thought how "Jack", cold-footed, useless swine,
Had panicked down the trench that night the mine
Went up at Wicked Corner; how he'd tried
To get sent home, and how, at last, he died,
Blown to small bits. And no one seemed to care
Except that lonely woman with white hair.

August 1916

Does not refer to anyone I have known. But it is pathetically true. And of course the 'average Englishman' will hate it. This, and 'The Tombstone-Maker', 'The One-Legged Man' and 'Arms and the Man', show a resemblance to Hardy's *Satires of Circumstance*, which I read with amusement in 1914, but now find unworthy of his greatness.

Stretcher Case

(TO EDWARD MARSH)

He woke; the clank and racket of the train
Kept time with angry throbbings in his brain.
Then for a while he lapsed and drowsed again.
At last he lifted his bewildered eyes
And blinked, and rolled them sidelong; hills and skies,
Heavily wooded, hot with August haze,
And, slipping backward, golden for his gaze,
Acres of harvest. Feebly now he drags
Exhausted ego back from glooms and quags
And blasting tumult, terror, hurtling glare,
To calm and brightness, havens of sweet air.
He sighed, confused; then drew a cautious breath;
This level journeying was no ride through death.
"If I were dead," he mused, "there'd be no thinking—
Only some plunging underworld of sinking,
And hueless, shifting welter where I'd drown."

Then he remembered that his name was Brown.

But was he back in Blighty? Slow he turned,
Till in his heart thanksgiving leapt and burned.
There shone the blue serene, the prosperous land,
Trees, cows and hedges; skipping these, he scanned
Large, friendly names, that change not with the year,
Lung Tonic, Mustard, Liver Pills and Beer.

August 1916

Written in hospital at Oxford.

The Road

The road is thronged with women; soldiers pass
And halt, but never see them; yet they're here—
A patient crowd along the sodden grass,
Silent, worn out with waiting, sick with fear.
The road goes crawling up a long hillside,
All ruts and stones and sludge, and the emptied dregs
Of battle thrown in heaps. Here where they died
Are stretched big-bellied horses with stiff legs,
And dead men, bloody-fingered from the fight,
Stare up at caverned darkness winking white.

You in the bomb-scorched kilt, poor sprawling Jock,
You tottered here and fell, and stumbled on,
Half dazed for want of sleep. No dream would mock
Your reeling brain with comforts lost and gone.
You did not feel her arms about your knees,
Her blind caress, her lips upon your head.
Too tired for thoughts of home and love and ease,
The road would serve you well enough for bed.

August 1916

This is the road through Mametz village as I saw it early in July 1916, when we struggled up through the mud to make a night attack on Quadrangle Trench.

The Death-Bed

He drowsed and was aware of silence heaped
Round him, unshaken as the steadfast walls;
Aqueous like floating rays of amber light,
Soaring and quivering in the wings of sleep.
Silence and safety; and his mortal shore
Lipped by the inward, moonless waves of death.

Someone was holding water to his mouth.
He swallowed, unresisting; moaned and dropped
Through crimson gloom to darkness; and forgot
The opiate throb and ache that was his wound.
    Water—calm, sliding green above the weir.
    Water—a sky-lit alley for his boat,
    Bird-voiced, and bordered with reflected flowers
    And shaken hues of summer; drifting down,
    He dipped contented oars, and sighed, and slept.

Night, with a gust of wind, was in the ward,
Blowing the curtain to a glimmering curve.
Night. He was blind; he could not see the stars
Glinting among the wraiths of wandering cloud;
Queer blots of colour, purple, scarlet, green,
Flickered and faded in his drowning eyes.

Rain—he could hear it rustling through the dark;
Fragrance and passionless music woven as one;
Warm rain on drooping roses; pattering showers
That soak the woods; not the harsh rain that sweeps
Behind the thunder, but a trickling peace,
Gently and slowly washing life away.

.   .   .

He stirred, shifting his body; then the pain
Leapt like a prowling beast, and gripped and tore
His groping dreams with grinding claws and fangs.
    But someone was beside him; soon he lay
    Shuddering because that evil thing had passed.
    And death, who'd stepped toward him, paused and stared.

Light many lamps and gather round his bed.
Lend him your eyes, warm blood, and will to live.
Speak to him; rouse him; you may save him yet.
He's young; he hated War; how should he die
When cruel old campaigners win safe through?

But death replied: "I choose him." So he went,
And there was silence in the summer night;
Silence and safety; and the veils of sleep.
Then, far away, the thudding of the guns.

Weirleigh, August 1916

A memory of hospital at Amiens and a canoe on the Cherwell. Refused
by the *Westminster* without comment.

The Tombstone-Maker

He primmed his loose red mouth and leaned his head
Against a sorrowing angel's breast, and said:
"You'd think so much bereavement would have made
Unusual big demands upon my trade.
The War comes cruel hard on some poor folk;
Unless the fighting stops I'll soon be broke."

He eyed the Cemetery across the road.
"There's scores of bodies out abroad, this while,
That should be here by rights. They little know'd
How they'd get buried in such wretched style."

I told him with a sympathetic grin,
That Germans boil dead soldiers down for fat;
And he was horrified. "What shameful sin!
O sir, that Christian souls should come to that!"

October 1916

Two Hundred Years After

Trudging by Corbie Ridge one winter's night,
(Unless old hearsay memories tricked his sight)
Along the pallid edge of the quiet sky
He watched a nosing lorry grinding on,
And straggling files of men; when these were gone,
A double limber and six mules went by,
Hauling the rations up through ruts and mud
To trench-lines digged two hundred years ago.
Then darkness hid them with a rainy scud,
And soon he saw the village lights below.

But when he'd told his tale, an old man said
That *he'd* seen soldiers pass along that hill;
"Poor silent things, they were the English dead
Who came to fight in France and got their fill."

October 1916

A Ballad

Have you heard the famous story of the Captain in the Blanks
Who was out for blood and glory in the service of his king?
When he'd served at home a year, in a quaking sweat of fear
He arrived at bloody Combles when the talk was all of Tanks.

So he stuck it for a week (of that time he loves to speak);
Then he out with his revolver and he brandished it on high;
In a solitary place, with a white and anxious face,
Swift he plugged a bullet in his foot, and hoped he wouldn't die.

Now the Captain's at the Depot, lame, but happy as a lark;
And in billets out in France the men who knew him tell the story
Of "the bloke that 'ad an accident when walking in the dark"—
While the Captain teaches raw recruits the way to blood and glory

25 October 1916

Text from manuscript.

"They"

The Bishop tells us: "When the boys come back
They will not be the same; for they'll have fought
In a just cause: they lead the last attack
On Anti-Christ; their comrades' blood has bought
New right to breed an honourable race,
They have challenged Death and dared him face to face."

"We're none of us the same!" the boys reply.
"For George lost both his legs; and Bill's stone blind;
Poor Jim's shot through the lungs and like to die;
And Bert's gone syphilitic: you'll not find
A chap who's served that hasn't found *some* change."
And the Bishop said: "The ways of God are strange!"

31 October 1916

Written at 40 Half Moon Street about 1 a.m. after a long evening with
Robbie Ross, More Adey and Roderick Meiklejohn. I was so sleepy I
could hardly keep my eyes open, but the thing just wrote itself. And
Eddie Marsh, when I showed it to him one wet morning (at 10 Downing
Street!), said: "It's *too* horrible." As I was walking back I actually met
"the Bishop" (of London) and he turned a mild shining gaze on me and
my M. C.

Decorated

I watched a jostling mob that surged and yelled,
And fought along the street to see their man:
Was it some drunken bully that they held
For justice—some poor thief who snatched and ran?

I asked a grinning news-boy, "What's the fun?"
"The beggar did for five of 'em!" said he.
"But if he killed them why's he let off free?"
I queried—"Most chaps swing for murdering *one*."
He screamed with joy; and told me, when he'd done—
"It's Corporal Stubbs, the Birmingham V.C.!"

November 1916

Text from manuscript.

Arms and the Man

Young Croesus went to pay his call
On Colonel Sawbones, Caxton Hall:
And, though his wound was healed and mended,
He hoped he'd get his leave extended.

The waiting-room was dark and bare.
He eyed a neat-framed notice there
Above the fireplace hung to show
Disabled heroes where to go

For arms and legs; with scale of price,
And words of dignified advice
How officers could get them free.

Elbow or shoulder, hip or knee,
Two arms, two legs, though all were lost,
They'd be restored him free of cost.
Then a Girl Guide looked in to say,
"Will Captain Croesus come this way?"

November 1916

A Mystic as Soldier

I lived my days apart,
Dreaming fair songs for God;
By the glory in my heart
Covered and crowned and shod.

Now God is in the strife,
And I must seek Him there,
Where death outnumbers life,
And fury smites the air.

I walk the secret way
With anger in my brain.
O music through my clay,
When will you sound again?

November 1916

The Poet as Hero

You've heard me, scornful, harsh, and discontented,
    Mocking and loathing War: you've asked me why
Of my old, silly sweetness I've repented—
    My ecstasies changed to an ugly cry.

You are aware that once I sought the Grail,
    Riding in armour bright, serene and strong;
And it was told that through my infant wail
    There rose immortal semblances of song.

But now I've said good-bye to Galahad,
    And am no more the knight of dreams and show:
For lust and senseless hatred make me glad,
    And my killed friends are with me where I go.
Wound for red wound I burn to smite their wrongs;
And there is absolution in my songs.

Published only in the *Cambridge Magazine*, 2 December 1916.

Secret Music

I keep such music in my brain
No din this side of death can quell;
Glory exulting over pain,
And beauty, garlanded in hell.

My dreaming spirit will not heed
The roar of guns that would destroy
My life that on the gloom can read
Proud-surging melodies of joy.

To the world's end I went, and found
Death in his carnival of glare;
But in my torment I was crowned,
And music dawned above despair.

December 1916

A Whispered Tale

(TO J.D.)

I'd heard fool-heroes brag of where they'd been,
With stories of the glories that they'd seen.
But you, good simple soldier, seasoned well
In woods and posts and crater-lines of hell
Who dodge remembered "crumps" with wry grimace,
Endured experience in your queer, kind face,
Fatigues and vigils haunting nerve-strained eyes,
And both your brothers killed to make you wise;
You had no babbling phrases; what you said
Was like a message from the maimed and dead.
But memory brought the voice I knew, whose note
Was muted when they shot you in the throat;
And still you whisper of the war, and find
Sour jokes for all those horrors left behind.

December 1916

Refers to Julian Dadd of C. Coy, First Royal Welch Fusiliers, who got hit in the neck at Ginchy on September 3, when his brother (who got the M.C.) was killed. His other brother was killed at Gallipoli, and his father, the black-and-white sporting artist, died in January 1917. The Dadds were great swimmers, and splendid fellows. J.D. was in a mental hospital in September 1917, but recovered later on.

The Distant Song

He stood in the gray trench and longed for home:
Chilled with the dreary morning and the rain,
He shivered, wondering if they'd soon stand down;
For he'd been getting wire out half the night,
And crawling round the craters on patrol.

There seemed no sort of comfort left in life;
Only a stupid greed for food and sleep,
And angry grudge against the filth and noise.
Stamping his feet, he knew he ought to go
And joke with huddling men about the Bosches—
"Hoping our big Trench-Mortars gave them hell."
    He listened to the tinkling drops of rain
    On his steel helmet; then he thought of roofs,
    And soldiers snug in billets, warm and clean.

Down by the splintered trees of Hidden Wood,
Beyond the German line a blackbird sang;
And suddenly he was aware of spring—
    So he stood staring from his ghastly ditch,
    While Paradise was in the distant song.

December 1916

Versified from a trench diary. A phrase or two used for end of *Fox-Hunting Man*.

Text from manuscript.

The March-Past

In red and gold the Corps-Commander stood,
With ribboned breast puffed out for all to see:
He'd sworn to beat the Germans, if he could;
For God had taught him strength and strategy.
He was our leader, and a judge of Port—
Rode well to hounds, and was a damned good sort.

"Eyes right!" We passed him with a jaunty stare.
 "Eyes front!" He'd watched his trusted legions go.
I wonder if he guessed how many there
Would get knocked out of time in next week's show.
"Eyes right!" The corpse-commander was a Mute;
And Death leered round him, taking our salute.

25 December 1916

Text from manuscript.

Enemies

He stood alone in some queer sunless place
Where Armageddon ends. Perhaps he longed
For days he might have lived; but his young face
Gazed forth untroubled: and suddenly there thronged
Round him the hulking Germans that I shot
When for his death my brooding rage was hot.

He stared at them, half-wondering; and then
They told him how I'd killed them for his sake—
Those patient, stupid, sullen ghosts of men;
And still there seemed no answer he could make.
At last he turned and smiled. One took his hand
Because his face could make them understand.

6 January 1917

When I'm among a Blaze of Lights

When I'm among a blaze of lights,
With tawdry music and cigars
And women dawdling through delights,
And officers in cocktail bars,
Sometimes I think of garden nights
And elm trees nodding at the stars.

I dream of a small firelit room
With yellow candles burning straight,
And glowing pictures in the gloom,
And kindly books that hold me late.
Of things like these I choose to think
When I can never be alone:
Then someone says "Another drink?"
And turns my living heart to stone.

8 January 1917

"Blighters"

The House is crammed: tier beyond tier they grin
And cackle at the Show, while prancing ranks
Of harlots shrill the chorus, drunk with din;
"We're sure the Kaiser loves our dear old Tanks!"

I'd like to see a Tank come down the stalls,
Lurching to ragtime tunes, or "Home, sweet Home",
And there'd be no more jokes in Music-halls
To mock the riddled corpses round Bapaume.

4 February 1917

Conscripts

"Fall in, that awkward squad, and strike no more
Attractive attitudes! Dress by the right!
The luminous rich colours that you wore
Have changed to hueless khaki in the night.
Magic? What's magic got to do with you?
There's no such thing! Blood's red, and skies are blue."

They gasped and sweated, marching up and down.
I drilled them till they cursed my raucous shout.
Love chucked his lute away and dropped his crown.
Rhyme got sore heels and wanted to fall out.
"Left, right! Press on your butts!" They looked at me
Reproachful; how I longed to set them free!

I gave them lectures on Defence, Attack;
They fidgeted and shuffled, yawned and sighed,
And boggled at my questions. Joy was slack,
And Wisdom gnawed his fingers, gloomy-eyed.
Young Fancy—how I loved him all the while—
Stared at his note-book with a rueful smile.

Their training done, I shipped them all to France,
Where most of those I'd loved too well got killed.
Rapture and pale Enchantment and Romance,
And many a sickly, slender lord who'd filled
My soul long since with lutanies of sin,
Went home, because they couldn't stand the din.

But the kind, common ones that I despised
(Hardly a man of them I'd count as friend),
What stubborn-hearted virtues they disguised!

They stood and played the hero to the end,
Won gold and silver medals bright with bars,
And marched resplendent home with crowns and stars.

Published in the *Spectator*, 17 February 1917.

Base Details

If I were fierce, and bald, and short of breath,
  I'd live with scarlet Majors at the Base,
And speed glum heroes up the line to death.
  You'd see me with my puffy petulant face,
Guzzling and gulping in the best hotel,
  Reading the Roll of Honour. "Poor young chap,"
I'd say—"I used to know his father well;
  Yes, we've lost heavily in this last scrap."
And when the war is done and youth stone dead,
I'd toddle safely home and die—in bed.

Rouen, 4 March 1917

In the Church of St Ouen

Time makes me be a soldier. But I know
That had I lived six hundred years ago
I might have tried to build within my heart
A church like this, where I could dwell apart
With chanting peace. My spirit longs for prayer;
And, lost to God, I seek him everywhere.
Here, where the windows burn and bloom like flowers,
And sunlight falls and fades with tranquil hours,
I could be half a saint, for like a rose
In heart-shaped stone the glory of Heaven glows.
But where I stand, desiring yet to stay,
Hearing rich music at the close of day,
The Spring Offensive (Easter is its date)
Calls me. And that's the music I await.

Rouen, 4 March 1917

Published only in *Siegfried Sassoon: Poet's Pilgrimage*, assembled by Dame
Felicitas Corrigan (1973). Text from manuscript.

Return

I have come home unnoticed; they are still;
No greetings pass between us; but they lie
Hearing the boom of guns along the hill,
Watching the flashes lick the glowering sky.

A wind of whispers comes from sightless faces;
"Have patience, and your bones shall share our bed."
Their voices haunt dark ways and ruined places,
Where once they spoke in deeds; who now are dead.

They wondered why I went; at last returning,
They guide my labouring feet through desolate mud.
And, choked with death, yet in their eyes discerning
My living strength; they are quickened in my blood.

11 March 1917

The Optimist

Down at the Base I listened to a throng
    Of subalterns "proceeding to the Front".
They hoped the show'd be finished before long,
    And cursed it for a senseless, bloody stunt.

But afterwards I had the luck to meet
    An optimist who vowed that all was well:
We'd "got the Germans absolutely beat",
    And he'd "come back to watch them getting hell".

"He wouldn't miss the end for worlds," he said . . .
    And then I saw his scar, and understood;
And asked if he'd been wounded in the head.
    He smiled—"A souvenir of Devil's Wood!"

Published only in the *Cambridge Magazine*, 21 April 1917.

The Rear-Guard

(HINDENBURG LINE, APRIL 1917)

Groping along the tunnel, step by step,
He winked his prying torch with patching glare
From side to side, and sniffed the unwholesome air.

Tins, boxes, bottles, shapes too vague to know;
A mirror smashed, the mattress from a bed;
And he, exploring fifty feet below
The rosy gloom of battle overhead.

Tripping, he grabbed the wall; saw some one lie
Humped at his feet, half-hidden by a rug,
And stooped to give the sleeper's arm a tug.
"I'm looking for headquarters." No reply.
"God blast your neck!" (For days he'd had no sleep)
"Get up and guide me through this stinking place."
Savage, he kicked a soft unanswering heap,
And flashed his beam across the livid face
Terribly glaring up, whose eyes yet wore
Agony dying hard ten days before;
And fists of fingers clutched a blackening wound.

Alone he staggered on until he found
Dawn's ghost that filtered down a shafted stair
To the dazed, muttering creatures underground
Who hear the boom of shells in muffled sound.
At last, with sweat of horror in his hair,

He climbed through darkness to the twilight air,
Unloading hell behind him step by step.

22 April 1917

Written at Denmark Hill Hospital about ten days after I was wounded.
Gosse, after seeing me there, wrote to Uncle Hamo that he thought I
was suffering from severe shock. But if so, could I have written such a
strong poem?

To the Warmongers

I'm back again from hell
With loathsome thoughts to sell;
Secrets of death to tell;
And horrors from the abyss.
Young faces bleared with blood,
Sucked down into the mud,
You shall hear things like this,
Till the tormented slain
Crawl round and once again,
With limbs that twist awry
Moan out their brutish pain,
As the fighters pass them by.
For you our battles shine
With triumph half-divine;
And the glory of the dead
Kindles in each proud eye.
But a curse is on my head,
That shall not be unsaid,
And the wounds in my heart are red,
For I have watched them die.

Denmark Hill Hospital, 23 April 1917

Text from manuscript.

The General

"Good-morning, good-morning!" the General said
When we met him last week on our way to the line.
Now the soldiers he smiled at are most of 'em dead,
And we're cursing his staff for incompetent swine.
"He's a cheery old card," grunted Harry to Jack
As they slogged up to Arras with rifle and pack.

                    .   .

But he did for them both by his plan of attack.

Denmark Hill Hospital, April 1917

The Hawthorn Tree

Not much to me is yonder lane
    Where I go every day;
But when there's been a shower of rain
    And hedge-birds whistle gay,
I know my lad that's out in France
    With fearsome things to see
Would give his eyes for just one glance
    At our white hawthorn tree.

       .   .   .

Not much to me is yonder lane
    Where *he* so longs to tread:
But when there's been a shower of rain
I think I'll never weep again
    Until I've heard he's dead.

25 May 1917

In an Underground Dressing-Station

Quietly they set their burden down: he tried
To grin; moaned; moved his head from side to side.

.   .   .

"O put my leg down, doctor, do!" (He'd got
A bullet in his ankle; and he'd been shot
Horribly through the guts.) The surgeon seemed
So kind and gentle, saying, above that crying,
"You *must* keep still, my lad." But he was dying.

2 June 1917 (begun in April)

Supreme Sacrifice

I told her our Battalion'd got a knock.
"Six officers were killed; a hopeless show!"
Her tired eyes half-confessed she'd felt the shock
Of ugly war brought home. And then a slow
Spiritual brightness stole across her face . . . .
"But *they* are safe and happy now," she said.
    I thought "The world's a silly sort of place
    When people think it's pleasant to be dead."
    I thought, "How cheery the brave troops would be
    If Sergeant-Majors taught Theosophy!"

2 June 1917

Published only in the *Cambridge Magazine*, 9 June 1917.

To Any Dead Officer

Well, how are things in Heaven? I wish you'd say,
   Because I'd like to know that you're all right.
Tell me, have you found everlasting day,
   Or been sucked in by everlasting night?
For when I shut my eyes your face shows plain;
   I hear you make some cheery old remark—
I can rebuild you in my brain,
   Though you've gone out patrolling in the dark.

You hated tours of trenches; you were proud
   Of nothing more than having good years to spend;
Longed to get home and join the careless crowd
   Of chaps who work in peace with Time for friend.
That's all washed out now. You're beyond the wire:
   No earthly chance can send you crawling back;
You've finished with machine-gun fire—
   Knocked over in a hopeless dud-attack.

Somehow I always thought you'd get done in,
   Because you were so desperate keen to live:
You were all out to try and save your skin,
   Well knowing how much the world had got to give.
You joked at shells and talked the usual "shop,"
   Stuck to your dirty job and did it fine:
With "Jesus Christ! when *will* it stop?
   Three years . . . It's hell unless we break their line."

So when they told me you'd been left for dead
    I wouldn't believe them, feeling it *must* be true.
Next week the bloody Roll of Honour said
    "Wounded and missing"—(That's the thing to do
When lads are left in shell-holes dying slow,
    With nothing but blank sky and wounds that ache,
Moaning for water till they know
    It's night, and then it's not worth while to wake!)

        .   .   .

Good-bye, old lad! Remember me to God,
    And tell Him that our Politicians swear
They won't give in till Prussian Rule's been trod
    Under the Heel of England . . . Are you there? . . .
Yes . . . and the War won't end for at least two years;
But we've got stacks of men . . . I'm blind with tears,
    Staring into the dark. Cheero!
I wish they'd killed you in a decent show.

Mid-June 1917

S.S. noted that the poem was addressed to Lieutenant E.L. Orme of the
Second Battalion, R.W.F., killed in action on 27 May 1917.

Repression of War Experience

Now light the candles; one; two; there's a moth;
What silly beggars they are to blunder in
And scorch their wings with glory, liquid flame—
No, no, not that,—it's bad to think of war,
When thoughts you've gagged all day come back to scare you;
And it's been proved that soldiers don't go mad
Unless they lose control of ugly thoughts
That drive them out to jabber among the trees.

Now light your pipe; look, what a steady hand.
Draw a deep breath; stop thinking; count fifteen,
And you're as right as rain . . . .
      Why won't it rain? . . .
I wish there'd be a thunder-storm to-night,
With bucketsful of water to sluice the dark,
And make the roses hang their dripping heads.

Books; what a jolly company they are,
Standing so quiet and patient on their shelves,
Dressed in dim brown, and black, and white, and green,
And every kind of colour. Which will you read?
Come on; O *do* read something; they're so wise.
I tell you all the wisdom of the world
Is waiting for you on those shelves; and yet
You sit and gnaw your nails, and let your pipe out,
And listen to the silence: on the ceiling
There's one big, dizzy moth that bumps and flutters;
And in the breathless air outside the house
The garden waits for something that delays.
There must be crowds of ghosts among the trees,—
Not people killed in battle—they're in France—
But horrible shapes in shrouds—old men who died

Slow, natural deaths—old men with ugly souls,
Who wore their bodies out with nasty sins.

.   .   .

You're quiet and peaceful, summering safe at home;
You'd never think there was a bloody war on! . . .
O yes, you would . . .why, you can hear the guns.
Hark! Thud, thud, thud,—quite soft . . . they never cease—
Those whispering guns—O Christ, I want to go out
And screech at them to stop—I'm going crazy;
I'm going stark, staring mad because of the guns.

Weirleigh, July 1917

The title was that of a lecture given by W.H.R. Rivers in 1917 and
reprinted in his book *Instinct and the Unconscious* (1920).

Lamentations

I found him in the guard-room at the Base.
From the blind darkness I had heard his crying
And blundered in. With puzzled, patient face
A sergeant watched him; it was no good trying
To stop it; for he howled and beat his chest.
And, all because his brother had gone west,
Raved at the bleeding war; his rampant grief
Moaned, shouted, sobbed, and choked, while he was kneelin
Half-naked on the floor. In my belief
Such men have lost all patriotic feeling.

Summer 1917 (episode at Rouen, February 1917)

The Effect

The effect of our bombardment was terrific. One man told me he had never seen so many dead before.—*War Correspondent*.

"He'd never seen so many dead before."
They sprawled in yellow daylight while he swore
And gasped and lugged his everlasting load
Of bombs along what once had been a road.
"How peaceful are the dead."
Who put that silly gag in someone's head?

"He'd never seen so many dead before."
The lilting words danced up and down his brain,
While corpses jumped and capered in the rain.
No, no; he wouldn't count them any more . . .
The dead have done with pain:
They've choked; they can't come back to life again.

When Dick was killed last week he looked like that,
Flapping along the fire-step like a fish,
After the blazing crump had knocked him flat . . .
*"How many dead? As many as ever you wish.
Don't count 'em; they're too many.
Who'll buy my nice fresh corpses, two a penny?"*

Summer 1917 (Hindenburg Line material)

Dreamers

Soldiers are citizens of death's grey land,
   Drawing no dividend from time's to-morrows.
In the great hour of destiny they stand,
   Each with his feuds, and jealousies, and sorrows.
Soldiers are sworn to action; they must win
   Some flaming, fatal climax with their lives.
Soldiers are dreamers; when the guns begin
   They think of firelit homes, clean beds and wives.

I see them in foul dug-outs, gnawed by rats,
   And in the ruined trenches, lashed with rain,
Dreaming of things they did with balls and bats,
   And mocked by hopeless longing to regain
Bank-holidays, and picture shows, and spats,
   And going to the office in the train.

Craiglockhart, 1917

Published in the hospital paper, the *Hydra*, 1 September 1917.

Editorial Impressions

He seemed so certain "all was going well",
As he discussed the glorious time he'd had
While visiting the trenches.
                "One can tell
You've gathered big impressions!" grinned the lad
Who'd been severely wounded in the back
In some wiped-out impossible Attack.
"Impressions? Yes, most vivid! I am writing
A little book called *Europe on the Rack*,
Based on notes made while witnessing the fighting.
I hope I've caught the feeling of 'the Line',
And the amazing spirit of the troops.
By Jove, those flying-chaps of ours are fine!
I watched one daring beggar looping loops,
Soaring and diving like some bird of prey.
And through it all I felt that splendour shine
Which makes us win."
                The soldier sipped his wine.
"Ah, yes, but it's the Press that leads the way!"

Craiglockhart, 1917

Published in the *Cambridge Magazine*, 22 September 1917.

Wirers

"Pass it along, the wiring party's going out"—
And yawning sentries mumble, "Wirers going out."
Unravelling; twisting; hammering stakes with muffled thud,
They toil with stealthy haste and anger in their blood.

The Bosche sends up a flare. Black forms stand rigid there,
Stock-still like posts; then darkness, and the clumsy ghosts
Stride hither and thither, whispering, tripped by
        clutching snare
Of snags and tangles.
                Ghastly dawn with vaporous coasts
Gleams desolate along the sky, night's misery ended.

Young Hughes was badly hit; I heard him carried away,
Moaning at every lurch; no doubt he'll die to-day.
But *we* can say the front-line wire's been safely mended.

Craiglockhart, 1917

Published in the *Hydra*, 29 September 1917.

Does it Matter?

Does it matter?—losing your legs? . . .
For people will always be kind,
And you need not show that you mind
When the others come in after hunting
To gobble their muffins and eggs.

Does it matter?—losing your sight? . . .
There's such splendid work for the blind;
And people will always be kind,
As you sit on the terrace remembering
And turning your face to the light.

Do they matter?—those dreams from the pit? . . .
You can drink and forget and be glad,
And people won't say that you're mad;
For they'll know that you've fought for your country
And no one will worry a bit.

Craiglockhart, 1917

Published in the *Cambridge Magazine*, 6 October 1917.

How to Die

Dark clouds are smouldering into red
    While down the craters morning burns.
The dying soldier shifts his head
    To watch the glory that returns;
He lifts his fingers toward the skies
    Where holy brightness breaks in flame;
Radiance reflected in his eyes,
    And on his lips a whispered name.

You'd think, to hear some people talk,
    That lads go west with sobs and curses,
And sullen faces white as chalk,
    Hankering for wreaths and tombs and hearses.
But they've been taught the way to do it
    Like Christian soldiers; not with haste
And shuddering groans; but passing through it
    With due regard for decent taste.

Craiglockhart, 1917

Published in the *Cambridge Magazine*, 6 October 1917.

The Fathers

Snug at the club two fathers sat,
Gross, goggle-eyed, and full of chat.
One of them said: "My eldest lad
Writes cheery letters from Bagdad.
But Arthur's getting all the fun
At Arras with his nine-inch gun."

"Yes," wheezed the other, "that's the luck!
My boy's quite broken-hearted, stuck
In England training all this year.
Still, if there's truth in what we hear,
The Huns intend to ask for more
     Before they bolt across the Rhine."
I watched them toddle through the door—
     Those impotent old friends of mine.

Craiglockhart, 1917

Published in the *Cambridge Magazine*, 13 October 1917.

Sick Leave

When I'm asleep, dreaming and lulled and warm,—
They come, the homeless ones, the noiseless dead.
While the dim charging breakers of the storm
Bellow and drone and rumble overhead,
Out of the gloom they gather about my bed.
   They whisper to my heart; their thoughts are mine.
   "Why are you here with all your watches ended?
   From Ypres to Frise we sought you in the Line."
In bitter safety I awake, unfriended;
And while the dawn begins with slashing rain
I think of the Battalion in the mud.
"When are you going out to them again?
Are they not still your brothers through our blood?"

Craiglockhart, 1917

Sent to Lady Ottoline Morrell on 17 October 1917. Published as
'Death's Brotherhood' in the *English Review*, January 1918.

Attack

At dawn the ridge emerges massed and dun
In wild purple of the glow'ring sun,
Smouldering through spouts of drifting smoke that shroud
The menacing scarred slope; and, one by one,
Tanks creep and topple forward to the wire.
The barrage roars and lifts. Then, clumsily bowed
With bombs and guns and shovels and battle-gear,
Men jostle and climb to meet the bristling fire.
Lines of grey, muttering faces, masked with fear,
They leave their trenches, going over the top,
While time ticks blank and busy on their wrists,
And hope, with furtive eyes and grappling fists,
Flounders in mud. O Jesus, make it stop!

Craiglockhart, 1917

From a note in my diary while observing the Hindenburg Line attack.

Fight to a Finish

The boys came back. Bands played and flags were flying,
　　And Yellow-Pressmen thronged the sunlit street
To cheer the soldiers who'd refrained from dying,
　　And hear the music of returning feet.
"Of all the thrills and ardours War has brought,
This moment is the finest." (So they thought.)

Snapping their bayonets on to charge the mob,
　　Grim Fusiliers broke ranks with glint of steel,
At last the boys had found a cushy job.

　　　　.　　　.　　　.

　　I heard the Yellow-Pressmen grunt and squeal;
And with my trusty bombers turned and went
To clear those Junkers out of Parliament.

Craiglockhart, 1917

Published in the *Cambridge Magazine*, 27 October 1917.

Survivors

No doubt they'll soon get well; the shock and strain
 Have caused their stammering, disconnected talk.
Of course they're "longing to go out again,"—
 These boys with old, scared faces, learning to walk.
They'll soon forget their haunted nights; their cowed
 Subjection to the ghosts of friends who died,—
Their dreams that drip with murder; and they'll be proud
 Of glorious war that shatter'd all their pride . . .
Men who went out to battle, grim and glad;
Children, with eyes that hate you, broken and mad.

Craiglockhart, October 1917

The Investiture

God with a Roll of Honour in His hand
Sits welcoming the heroes who have died,
While sorrowless angels ranked on either side
Stand easy in Elysium's meadow-land.
Then *you* come shyly through the garden gate,
Wearing a blood-soaked bandage on your head;
And God says something kind because you're dead,
And homesick, discontented with your fate.

If I were there we'd snowball Death with skulls;
Or ride away to hunt in Devil's Wood
With ghosts of puppies that we walked of old.
But you're alone; and solitude annuls
Our earthly jokes; and strangely wise and good
You roam forlorn along the streets of gold.

Craiglockhart, 1917

Published in the *Cambridge Magazine*, 3 November 1917.

Thrushes

Tossed on the glittering air they soar and skim,
Whose voices make the emptiness of light
A windy palace. Quavering from the brim
Of dawn, and bold with song at edge of night,
They clutch their leafy pinnacles and sing
Scornful of man, and from his toils aloof
Whose heart's a haunted woodland whispering;
Whose thoughts return on tempest-baffled wing;
Who hears the cry of God in everything,
And storms the gate of nothingness for proof.

Craiglockhart, 1917

Published in the *Hydra*, November 1917.

Glory of Women

You love us when we're heroes, home on leave,
Or wounded in a mentionable place.
You worship decorations; you believe
That chivalry redeems the war's disgrace.
You make us shells. You listen with delight,
By tales of dirt and danger fondly thrilled.
You crown our distant ardours while we fight,
And mourn our laurelled memories when we're killed.
You can't believe that British troops "retire"
When hell's last horror breaks them, and they run,
Trampling the terrible corpses—blind with blood.
    O German mother dreaming by the fire,
While you are knitting socks to send your son
His face is trodden deeper in the mud.

Craiglockhart, 1917

Published in the *Cambridge Magazine*, 8 December 1917.

Their Frailty

He's got a Blighty wound. He's safe; and then
    War's fine and bold and bright.
She can forget the doomed and prisoned men
    Who agonize and fight.

He's back in France. She loathes the listless strain
    And peril of his plight,
Beseeching Heaven to send him home again,
    She prays for peace each night.

Husbands and sons and lovers; everywhere
    They die; War bleeds us white.
Mothers and wives and sweethearts,—they don't care
    So long as He's all right.

Craiglockhart, 1917

Published in the *Cambridge Magazine*, 8 December 1917.

Break of Day

There seemed a smell of autumn in the air
At the bleak end of night; he shivered there
In a dank, musty dug-out where he lay,
Legs wrapped in sandbags,—lumps of chalk and clay
Spattering his face. Dry-mouthed, he thought, "To-day
We start the damned attack; and, Lord knows why,
Zero's at nine; how bloody if I'm done in
Under the freedom of that morning sky!"
And then he coughed and dozed, cursing the din.

Was it the ghost of autumn in that smell
Of underground, or God's blank heart grown kind,
That sent a happy dream to him in hell?—
Where men are crushed like clods, and crawl to find
Some crater for their wretchedness; who lie
In outcast immolation, doomed to die
Far from clean things or any hope of cheer,
Cowed anger in their eyes, till darkness brims
And roars into their heads, and they can hear
Old childish talk, and tags of foolish hymns.

He sniffs the chilly air; (his dreaming starts),
He's riding in a dusty Sussex lane
In quiet September; slowly night departs;
And he's a living soul, absolved from pain.
Beyond the brambled fences where he goes
Are glimmering fields with harvest piled in sheaves,
And tree-tops dark against the stars grown pale;
Then, clear and shrill, a distant farm-cock crows;
And there's a wall of mist along the vale
Where willows shake their watery-sounding leaves,
He gazes on it all, and scarce believes

That earth is telling its old peaceful tale;
He thanks the blessed world that he was born . . .
Then, far away, a lonely note of the horn.

They're drawing the Big Wood! Unlatch the gate,
And set Golumpus going on the grass;
He knows the corner where it's best to wait
And hear the crashing woodland chorus pass;
The corner where old foxes make their track
To the Long Spinney; that's the place to be.
The bracken shakes below an ivied tree,
And then a cub looks out; and "Tally-o-back!"
He bawls, and swings his thong with volleying crack,—
All the clean thrill of autumn in his blood,
And hunting surging through him like a flood
In joyous welcome from the untroubled past;
While the war drifts away, forgotten at last.

Now a red, sleepy sun above the rim
Of twilight stares along the quiet weald,
And the kind, simple country shines revealed
In solitudes of peace, no longer dim.
The old horse lifts his face and thanks the light,
Then stretches down his head to crop the green.
All things that he has loved are in his sight;
The places where his happiness has been
Are in his eyes, his heart, and they are good.

.   .   .

Hark! there's the horn: they're drawing the Big Wood.

Craiglockhart, 1917

Published in the *Hydra*, December 1917.

Prelude: The Troops

Dim, gradual thinning of the shapeless gloom
Shudders to drizzling daybreak that reveals
Disconsolate men who stamp their sodden boots
And turn dulled, sunken faces to the sky
Haggard and hopeless. They, who have beaten down
The stale despair of night, must now renew
Their desolation in the truce of dawn,
Murdering the livid hours that grope for peace.

Yet these who cling to life with stubborn hands,
Can grin through storms of death and find a gap
In the clawed, cruel tangles of his defence.
They march from safety, and the bird-sung joy
Of grass-green thickets, to the land where all
Is ruin, and nothing blossoms but the sky
That hastens over them where they endure
Sad, smoking, flat horizons, reeking woods,
And foundered trench-lines volleying doom for doom.

O my brave brown companions, when your souls
Flock silently away, and the eyeless dead
Shame the wild beast of battle on the ridge,
Death will stand grieving in that field of war
Since your unvanquished hardihood is spent.
And through some mooned Valhalla there will pass
Battalions and battalions, scarred from hell;
The unreturning army that was youth;
The legions who have suffered and are dust.

Craiglockhart, 1917

Counter-Attack

We'd gained our first objective hours before
While dawn broke like a face with blinking eyes,
Pallid, unshaved and thirsty, blind with smoke.
Things seemed all right at first. We held their line,
With bombers posted, Lewis guns well placed,
And clink of shovels deepening the shallow trench.
　　The place was rotten with dead; green clumsy legs
　　High-booted, sprawled and grovelled along the saps
　　And trunks, face downward, in the sucking mud,
　　Wallowed like trodden sand-bags loosely filled;
　　And naked sodden buttocks, mats of hair,
　　Bulged, clotted heads slept in the plastering slime.
　　And then the rain began,—the jolly old rain!

A yawning soldier knelt against the bank,
Staring across the morning blear with fog;
He wondered when the Allemands would get busy;
And then, of course, they started with five-nines
Traversing, sure as fate, and never a dud.
Mute in the clamour of shells he watched them burst
Spouting dark earth and wire with gusts from hell,
While posturing giants dissolved in drifts of smoke.
He crouched and flinched, dizzy with galloping fear,
Sick for escape,—loathing the strangled horror
And butchered, frantic gestures of the dead.

An officer came blundering down the trench:
"Stand-to and man the fire-step!" On he went . . .
Gasping and bawling, "Fire-step . . .counter-attack!"
Then the haze lifted. Bombing on the right
Down the old sap: machine-guns on the left;
And stumbling figures looming out in front.

"O Christ, they're coming at us!" Bullets spat,
And he remembered his rifle . . . rapid fire . . .
And started blazing wildly . . . then a bang
Crumpled and spun him sideways, knocked him out
To grunt and wriggle: none heeded him; he choked
And fought the flapping veils of smothering gloom,
Lost in a blurred confusion of yells and groans . . .
Down, and down, and down, he sank and drowned,
Bleeding to death. The counter-attack had failed.

Craiglockhart, 1917 (from a July 1916 draft)

Twelve Months After

Hullo! here's my platoon, the lot I had last year.
"The war'll be over soon."
                        "What 'opes?"
                                "No bloody fear!"
Then, "Number Seven, 'shun! All present and correct."
They're standing in the sun, impassive and erect.
Young Gibson with his grin; and Morgan, tired and white;
Jordan, who's out to win a D.C.M. some night;
And Hughes that's keen on wiring; and Davies ('79),
Who always must be firing at the Bosche front line.

              .   .   .

"Old soldiers never die; they simply fide a-why!"
That's what they used to sing along the roads last spring;
That's what they used to say before the push began;
That's where they are to-day, knocked over to a man.

Craiglockhart, 1917

Banishment

I am banished from the patient men who fight.
They smote my heart to pity, built my pride.
Shoulder to aching shoulder, side by side,
They trudged away from life's broad wealds of light.
Their wrongs were mine; and ever in my sight
They went arrayed in honour. But they died,—
Not one by one: and mutinous I cried
To those who sent them out into the night.

The darkness tells how vainly I have striven
To free them from the pit where they must dwell
In outcast gloom convulsed and jagged and riven
By grappling guns. Love drove me to rebel.
Love drives me back to grope with them through hell;
And in their tortured eyes I stand forgiven.

Craiglockhart, 1917

Autumn

October's bellowing anger breaks and cleaves
The bronzed battalions of the stricken wood
In whose lament I hear a voice that grieves
For battle's fruitless harvest, and the feud
Of outraged men. Their lives are like the leaves
Scattered in flocks of ruin, tossed and blown
Along the westering furnace flaring red.
O martyred youth and manhood overthrown,
The burden of your wrongs is on my head.

Craiglockhart, 1917

In Barracks

The Barrack-square, washed clean with rain,
Shines wet and wintry-grey and cold.
Young Fusiliers, strong-legged and bold,
March and wheel and march again.
The sun looks over the barrack gate,
Warm and white with glaring shine,
To watch the soldiers of the Line
That life has hired to fight with fate.

Fall out: the long parades are done.
Up comes the dark; down goes the sun.
The square is walled with windowed light.
Sleep well, you lusty Fusiliers;
Shut your brave eyes on sense and sight,
And banish from your dreamless ears
The bugle's dying notes that say,
"Another night; another day."

Limerick, 9 January 1918

The Dream

I

Moonlight and dew-drenched blossom, and the scent
Of summer gardens; these can bring you all
Those dreams that in the starlit silence fall:
Sweet songs are full of odours.
                    While I went
Last night in drizzling dusk along a lane,
I passed a squalid farm; from byre and midden
Came the rank smell that brought me once again
A dream of war that in the past was hidden.

II

Up a disconsolate straggling village street
I saw the tired troops trudge: I heard their feet.
The cheery Q.M.S. was there to meet
And guide our Company in . . . .
                    I watched them stumble
Into some crazy hovel, too beat to grumble;
Saw them file inward, slipping from their backs
Rifles, equipment, packs.
On filthy straw they sit in the gloom, each face
Bowed to patched, sodden boots they must unlace,
While the wind chills their sweat through chinks and cracks.

III

I'm looking at their blistered feet; young Jones
Stares up at me, mud-splashed and white and jaded;
Out of his eyes the morning light has faded.
Old soldiers with three winters in their bones
Puff their damp Woodbines, whistle, stretch their toes:

They can still grin at me, for each of 'em knows
That I'm as tired as they are . . . .

                         Can they guess
The secret burden that is always mine?—
Pride in their courage; pity for their distress;
And burning bitterness
That I must take them to the accursèd Line.

IV

I cannot hear their voices, but I see
Dim candles in the barn: they gulp their tea,
And soon they'll sleep like logs. Ten miles away
The battle winks and thuds in blundering strife.
And I must lead them nearer, day by day,
To the foul beast of war that bludgeons life.

Limerick, 17 January 1918

Dead Musicians

From you, Beethoven, Bach, Mozart,
  The substance of my dreams took fire.
You built cathedrals in my heart,
  And lit my pinnacled desire.
You were the ardour and the bright
  Procession of my thoughts toward prayer.
You were the wrath of storm, the light
  On distant citadels aflare.

II

Great names, I cannot find you now
  In these loud years of youth that strives
Through doom toward peace: upon my brow
  I wear a wreath of banished lives.
You have no part with lads who fought
  And laughed and suffered at my side.
Your fugues and symphonies have brought
  No memory of my friends who died.

III

For when my brain is on their track,
In slangy speech I call them back.
With fox-trot tunes their ghosts I charm.
"Another little drink won't do us any harm."
  I think of ragtime; a bit of ragtime;
  And see their faces crowding round
  To the sound of the syncopated beat.

They've got such jolly things to tell,
Home from hell with a Blighty wound so neat . . .

.   .   .

And so the song breaks off; and I'm alone.
They're dead . . . For God's sake stop that gramophone.

Limerick, 19 January 1918

Together

Splashing along the boggy woods all day,
And over brambled hedge and holding clay,
I shall not think of him:
But when the watery fields grow brown and dim,
And hounds have lost their fox, and horses tire,
I know that he'll be with me on my way
Home through the darkness to the evening fire.

He's jumped each stile along the glistening lanes;
His hand will be upon the mud-soaked reins;
Hearing the saddle creak,
He'll wonder if the frost will come next week.
I shall forget him in the morning light;
And while we gallop on he will not speak:
But at the stable-door he'll say good-night.

Limerick, 30 January 1918

Invocation

Come down from heaven to meet me when my breath
Chokes, and through drumming shafts of stifling death
I stumble toward escape, to find the door
Opening on morn where I may breathe once more
Clear cock-crow airs across some valley dim
With whispering trees. While dawn along the rim
Of night's horizon flows in lakes of fire,
Come down from heaven's bright hill, my song's desire.

Belov'd and faithful, teach my soul to wake
In glades deep-ranked with flowers that gleam and shake
And flock your paths with wonder. In your gaze
Show me the vanquished vigil of my days.
Mute in that golden silence hung with green,
Come down from heaven and bring me in your eyes
Remembrance of all beauty that has been,
And stillness from the pools of Paradise.

Limerick, January 1918

Memory

When I was young my heart and head were light,
And I was gay and feckless as a colt
Out in the fields, with morning in the may,
Wind on the grass, wings in the orchard bloom.
    O thrilling sweet, my joy, when life was free
    And all the paths led on from hawthorn-time
    Across the carolling meadows into June.

But now my heart is heavy-laden. I sit
Burning my dreams away beside the fire:
For death has made me wise and bitter and strong;
And I am rich in all that I have lost.
    O starshine on the fields of long-ago,
    Bring me the darkness and the nightingale;
    Dim wealds of vanished summer, peace of home,
    And silence; and the faces of my friends.

Limerick, 1 February 1918

Remorse

Lost in the swamp and welter of the pit,
He flounders off the duck-boards; only he knows
Each flash and spouting crash,—each instant lit
When gloom reveals the streaming rain. He goes
Heavily, blindly on. And, while he blunders,
"Could anything be worse than this?"—he wonders,
Remembering how he saw those Germans run,
Screaming for mercy among the stumps of trees:
Green-faced, they dodged and darted: there was one
Livid with terror, clutching at his knees . . .
Our chaps were sticking 'em like pigs . . . "O hell!"
He thought—"there's things in war one dare not tell
Poor father sitting safe at home, who reads
Of dying heroes and their deathless deeds."

Limerick, 4 February 1918

118

Suicide in the Trenches

I knew a simple soldier boy
Who grinned at life in empty joy,
Slept soundly through the lonesome dark,
And whistled early with the lark.

In winter trenches, cowed and glum,
With crumps and lice and lack of rum,
He put a bullet through his brain.
No one spoke of him again.

.   .   .

You smug-faced crowds with kindling eye
Who cheer when soldier lads march by,
Sneak home and pray you'll never know
The hell where youth and laughter go.

Published in the *Cambridge Magazine*, 23 February 1918.

Concert Party

(EGYPTIAN BASE CAMP)

They are gathering round . . . .
Out of the twilight; over the grey-blue sand,
Shoals of low-jargoning men drift inward to the sound—
The jangle and throb of a piano . . . tum-ti-tum . . .
Drawn by a lamp, they come
Out of the glimmering lines of their tents, over the shuffling sand.

O sing us the songs, the songs of our own land,
You warbling ladies in white.
Dimness conceals the hunger in our faces,
This wall of faces risen out of the night,
These eyes that keep their memories of the places
So long beyond their sight.

Jaded and gay, the ladies sing; and the chap in brown
Tilts his grey hat; jaunty and lean and pale,
He rattles the keys . . . some actor-bloke from town . . .
God send you home; and then *A long, long trail;*
I hear you calling me; and *Dixieland* . . . .
Sing slowly . . . now the chorus . . . one by one
We hear them, drink them; till the concert's done.
Silent, I watch the shadowy mass of soldiers stand.
Silent, they drift away, over the glimmering sand.

Kantara, April 1918

Night on the Convoy

(ALEXANDRIA—MARSEILLES)

Out in the blustering darkness, on the deck
A gleam of stars looks down. Long blurs of black,
The lean Destroyers, level with our track,
Plunging and stealing, watch the perilous way
Through backward racing seas and caverns of chill spray.
One sentry by the davits, in the gloom
Stands mute: the boat heaves onward through the night.
Shrouded is every chink of cabined light:
And sluiced by floundering waves that hiss and boom
And crash like guns, the troop-ship shudders . . . doom.

Now something at my feet stirs with a sigh;
And slowly growing used to groping dark,
I know that the hurricane-deck down all its length,
Is heaped and spread with lads in sprawling strength—
Blanketed soldiers sleeping. In the stark
Danger of life at war, they lie so still,
All prostrate and defenceless, head by head . . .
And I remember Arras, and that hill
Where dumb with pain I stumbled among the dead.

We are going home. The troop-ship, in a thrill
Of fiery-chamber'd anguish, throbs and rolls.
We are going home . . . victims . . . three thousand souls.

May 1918

Reward

Months and weeks and days go past,
And my soldiers fall at last.
Months and weeks and days
Their ways must be my ways.
And evermore
Love guards the door.

From their eyes the gift I gain
Of grace that can subdue my pain:
From their eyes I hoard
My reward . . . .
O brothers in my striving, it were best
That I should share your rest.

5 June 1918

Text from manuscript.

I Stood with the Dead

I stood with the Dead, so forsaken and still:
When dawn was grey I stood with the Dead.
And my slow heart said, "You must kill, you must kill:
"Soldier, soldier, morning is red".

On the shapes of the slain in their crumpled disgrace
I stared for a while through the thin cold rain . . .
"O lad that I loved, there is rain on your face,
"And your eyes are blurred and sick like the plain."

I stood with the Dead. . . . They were dead; they were dead;
My heart and my head beat a march of dismay:
And gusts of the wind came dulled by the guns.
"Fall in!" I shouted; "Fall in for your pay!"

Habarcq, 18 June 1918

Trench Duty

Shaken from sleep, and numbed and scarce awake,
Out in the trench with three hours' watch to take,
I blunder through the splashing mirk; and then
Hear the gruff muttering voices of the men
Crouching in cabins candle-chinked with light.
Hark! There's the big bombardment on our right
Rumbling and bumping; and the dark's a glare
Of flickering horror in the sectors where
We raid the Bosche; men waiting, stiff and chilled,
Or crawling on their bellies through the wire.
"What? Stretcher-bearers wanted? Some one killed?"
Five minutes ago I heard a sniper fire:
Why did he do it? . . . Starlight overhead—
Blank stars. I'm wide-awake; and some chap's dead.

Published in *Counter-Attack*, 27 June 1918.

Joy-Bells

Ring your sweet bells; but let them be farewells
   To the green-vista'd gladness of the past
That changed us into soldiers; swing your bells
   To a joyful chime; but let it be the last.

What means this metal in windy belfries hung
   When guns are all our need? Dissolve these bells
Whose tones are tuned for peace: with martial tongue
   Let them cry doom and storm the sun with shells.

Bells are like fierce-browed prelates who proclaim
   That "if Our Lord returned He'd fight for *us*."
So let our bells and bishops do the same,
   Shoulder to shoulder with the motor-bus.

Published in *Counter-Attack*, 27 June 1918.

Song-Books of the War

In fifty years, when peace outshines
Remembrance of the battle lines,
Adventurous lads will sigh and cast
Proud looks upon the plundered past.
On summer morn or winter's night,
Their hearts will kindle for the fight,
Reading a snatch of soldier-song,
Savage and jaunty, fierce and strong;
And through the angry marching rhymes
Of blind regret and haggard mirth,
They'll envy us the dazzling times
When sacrifice absolved our earth.

Some ancient man with silver locks
Will lift his weary face to say:
"War was a fiend who stopped our clocks
Although we met him grim and gay."
And then he'll speak of Haig's last drive,
Marvelling that any came alive
Out of the shambles that men built
And smashed, to cleanse the world of guilt.
But the boys, with grin and sidelong glance,
Will think, "Poor grandad's day is done."
And dream of lads who fought in France
And lived in time to share the fun.

Published in *Counter-Attack*, 27 June 1918.

The Triumph

When life was a cobweb of stars for Beauty who came
    In the whisper of leaves or a bird's lone cry in the glen,
On dawn-lit hills and horizons girdled with flame
    I sought for the triumph that troubles the faces of men.

With death in the terrible flickering gloom of the fight
    I was cruel and fierce with despair; I was naked and bound;
I was stricken: and Beauty returned through the shambles of night;
    In the faces of men she returned; and their triumph I found.

Published in *Counter-Attack*, 27 June 1918.

Battalion-Relief

"Fall in! Now get a move on." (Curse the rain.)
We splash away along the straggling village,
Out to the flat rich country, green with June . . .
And sunset flares across wet crops and tillage,
Blazing with splendour-patches. (Harvest soon,
Up in the Line.) *"Perhaps the War'll be done*
"By Christmas-Day. Keep smiling then, old son."

Here's the Canal: it's dusk; we cross the bridge.
"Lead on there, by platoons." (The Line's a-glare
With shell-fire through the poplars; distant rattle
Of rifles and machine-guns.) *"Fritz is there!*
"Christ, ain't it lively, Sergeant? Is't a battle?"
More rain: the lightning blinks, and thunder rumbles.
"There's overhead artillery!" some chap grumbles.

What's all this mob at the cross-roads? Where are the
        guides? . . .
"Lead on with Number One." And off they go.
"Three minute intervals." (Poor blundering files,
Sweating and blindly burdened; who's to know
If death will catch them in those two dark miles?)
More rain. "Lead on, Headquarters." (That's the lot.)
"Who's that? . . . Oh, Sergeant-Major, don't get shot!
"And tell me, have we won this war or not?"

July 1918

128

The Dug-Out

Why do you lie with your legs ungainly huddled,
And one arm bent across your sullen, cold,
Exhausted face? It hurts my heart to watch you,
Deep-shadow'd from the candle's guttering gold;
And you wonder why I shake you by the shoulder;
Drowsy, you mumble and sigh and turn your head . . .
You are too young to fall asleep for ever;
And when you sleep you remind me of the dead.

St Venant, July 1918

Letter to Robert Graves

24 July 1918

American Red Cross Hospital, No. 22
98–99 Lancaster Gate, W.2

Dear Roberto,
I'd timed my death in action to the minute
(The *Nation* with my deathly verses in it).[1]
The day told off—13—(the month July)—
The picture planned—O Threshold of the dark!
And then, the quivering songster failed to die
Because the bloody Bullet missed its mark.

Here I am; they *would* send me back—
Kind M.O. at Base; Sassoon's morale grown slack;
Swallowed all his proud high thoughts and acquiesced.
O Gate of Lancaster, O Blightyland the Blessed.

No visitors allowed
Since Friends arrived in crowd—
Jabber—Gesture—Jabber—Gesture—Nerves went phut and
    failed
After the first afternoon when MarshMoonStreetMeiklejohn
    ArdoursandenduranSitwellitis prevailed,[2]
Caused complications and set my brain a-hop;
Sleeplessexasperuicide, O Jesu make it stop!

---

[1] 'I Stood with the Dead' (see p. 123), which appeared in the *Nation* on
13 July.

[2] Visits from Eddie Marsh, Robbie Ross (who lived in Half Moon Street),
Roderick Meiklejohn, Robert Nichols (whose first book of poems was
called *Ardours and Endurances*) and Osbert Sitwell.

But yesterday afternoon my reasoning Rivers[3] ran solemnly in,
With peace in the pools of his spectacled eyes and a wisely
      omnipotent grin;
And I fished in that steady grey stream and decided that I
After all am no longer the Worm that refuses to die.
But a gallant and glorious lyrical soldjer;
   Bolder and bolder; as he gets older;
   Shouting "Back to the Front
   For a scrimmaging Stunt."
   (I wish the weather wouldn't keep on getting colder.)

Yes, you can touch my Banker when you need him.
Why keep a Jewish friend unless you bleed him?

Oh yes, he's doing very well and sleeps from Two till Four.
And there was Jolly Otterleen[4] a knocking at the door,
But Matron says she mustn't, not however loud she knocks
(Though she's bags of golden Daisies and some Raspberries in a
      box),
Be admitted to the wonderful and wild and wobbly-witted
      sarcastic soldier-poet with a plaster on his crown,
Who pretends he doesn't know it (he's the Topic of the Town).

My God, my God, I'm so excited; I've just had a letter
From Stable who's commanding the Twenty-Fifth Battalion.

---

[3] Dr W. H. R. Rivers, FRS (1864–1922), psychologist and anthropo-
logist, Fellow of St John's College, Cambridge, was now a temporary
captain in the Royal Army Medical Corps. He had looked after S.S.
at Craiglockhart (see *Sherston's Progress* and *Siegfried's Journey*) and had
in many ways taken the place of the father S.S. had scarcely known.
[4] Lady Ottoline Morrell.

And my company, he tells me, doing better and better,
Pinched six Saxons after lunch,
And bagged machine-guns by the bunch.

But I—wasn't there—
O blast it isn't fair,
Because they'll all be wondering why
Dotty Captain wasn't standing by
When they came marching home.

But I don't care; I made them love me
Although they didn't want to do it, and I've sent them a
    glorious Gramophone and God send you back to me[5]
Over the green eviscerating sea—
And I'm ill and afraid to go back to them because those
    five-nines are so damned awful.
When you think of them all bursting and you're lying on your
    bed,
With the books you loved and longed for on the table; and your
    head
All crammed with village verses about Daffodils and Geese—
. . . O Jesu make it cease . . . .

O Rivers please take me. And make me
Go back to the war till it break me.
Some day my brain will go BANG,
And they'll say what lovely faces were
The soldier-lads he sang

Does this break your heart? What do I care?

                              Sassons[6]

---

[5] 'You made me love you: I didn't want to do it' and 'God send you
back to me' were popular songs of the day.
[6] One of the nicknames by which S. S. was known in the Army.

Published in a garbled and incomplete form in the first printing of *Good-Bye to All That* by Robert Graves (1929). Sassoon objected; the edition was withdrawn and reissued without the poem. Later that year it was pirated in an edition of fifty copies entitled *A Suppressed Poem*. This text is from the original manuscript letter.

Great Men

The great ones of the earth
Approve, with smiles and bland salutes, the rage
And monstrous tyranny they have brought to birth.
The great ones of the earth
Are much concerned about the wars they wage,
And quite aware of what those wars are worth.

You Marshals, gilt and red,
You Ministers and Princes, and Great Men,
Why can't you keep your mouthings for the dead?
Go round the simple cemeteries; and then
Talk of our noble sacrifice and losses
To the wooden crosses.

Published only in the *Cambridge Magazine*, 17 August 1918.

Trade Boycott

General Currycombe (half-pay)
Toddles round, and day by day
Swears he'll boycott (if he can)
German merchants, to a man!

He's a list in his fist
For the neighbourhood to sign.
"Only those", he thinks, "who do
To the Bull-dog breed are true. . . ."
But the signatures are few;
And he hasn't asked for mine.

Published only in the *Cambridge Magazine*, 14 September 1918.

Reconciliation

When you are standing at your hero's grave,
Or near some homeless village where he died,
Remember, through your heart's rekindling pride,
The German soldiers who were loyal and brave.

Men fought like brutes; and hideous things were done
And you have nourished hatred harsh and blind.
But in that Golgotha perhaps you'll find
The mothers of the men who killed your son.

November 1918

Memorial Tablet

(GREAT WAR)

Squire nagged and bullied till I went to fight,
(Under Lord Derby's Scheme). I died in hell—
(They called it Passchendaele). My wound was slight,
And I was hobbling back; and then a shell
Burst slick upon the duck-boards: so I fell
Into the bottomless mud, and lost the light.

At sermon-time, while Squire is in his pew,
He gives my gilded name a thoughtful stare;
For, though low down upon the list, I'm there;
"In proud and glorious memory" . . . that's my due.
Two bleeding years I fought in France, for Squire:
I suffered anguish that he's never guessed.
Once I came home on leave: and then went west . . .
What greater glory could a man desire?

November 1918

A Last Word

I

By Jove, I haven't seen you since the War!
I'm going to hurt your feelings: do you mind?

You'd got the best of me when last we met.
Though over forty, you were grand at games;
And I was under thirty, and a dud.
In all the affairs of life you had the laugh of me;
You, with your cricket Blue; and I with nothing
But anger at the world. You always stood
For institutions; read the *Morning Post*,
And thought Imperially—And when you bowled
You got me out. I wasn't in the picture
When men like you discussed the things that count.

Hardy, if you regarded him at all,
Was "a pernicious writer". And the Strikes
Made you feel insecure: you hated Labour—
Those roaring crowds at Cup-ties in the North.

I liked you; all my motives were confused;
I'd never tested yours; and you were just
Cheery and commonplace, but good at games;
And we were alien types who'd never clashed.

II

Now, when the winter of long War is past,
We meet again; and you are glad to see me.
You grasp my hand; observing that I wear
Three wound stripes and a Military Cross.
You've not the faintest doubt I've done my bit;
Your only wonder is that I'm alive.

If I'd refused to fight, if I had done
Two years hard labour, four years on the rack,
Instead of serving on the Western Front,
You'd meet me with contempt; you'd think of me
As an unspeakable blighter; you'd insult me
And feel you'd acted finely. (Afterwards,
You'd think of bitter things you might have said—
Things that you couldn't think of at the time . . .
I've felt like that myself when I've been angry.)

III

What have you done in the Great War, old man?
Four years' home-service, twenty miles from home,
Drawing a Major's pay. You've helped recruiting;
Drilled men for battle; won your spurs with pride;
Sat on court-martials; judged and sentenced soldiers;
And some of them have died to keep you snug.

IV

You're just the man you were four years ago;
You're looking fit and well; you've stuck it fine!
You want Protection; and you don't believe
In Leagues of Nations that include the Hun.
We're winning; you're more pleased than when we beat
The Boers, or won the rubber in the Tests.

V

I'm careful while I talk to you—quite careful;
I'm feeling slightly awkward: that's because
I can't speak easily about the War.
I ask you guarded questions, naming men
Who've come through safe and sound; and when we hit

On someone who's been killed or badly maimed,
We're silent for a while, and prod the ground.
I can talk safely of 'before the war,'
But that's a scrap-heap.
                    You must understand
I've got the laugh of you; I've got you beat,
Although I'm too well-bred to rub it in,
(As you'd be rubbing it in if I'd kept safe,
Or found high moral courage, and refused
To fight at all.)
                    Yet I remember men
Far grayer than you, that served with me in France—
Tough chaps, who went there of their own accord,
With no prestige to get them easy jobs . . .
But they were soldiers.
                    Well, we've clashed at last.
Good-bye. I hope they'll put you on to bowl!

Published only in the *Cambridge Magazine*, 18 January 1919.

Vicarious Christ

The Bishop of Byegumb was an old friend of our General;
In fact he knew him out in the Soudan.
He preached to our Brigade; and the impression that he made
Was astounding; he was such a Christian man.

He compared us to the martyrs who were burnt alive and
strangled;
O, it made us love the war—to hear him speak!
"The Americans," he said, "are coming over in large numbers;"
"And the Huns are getting weaker every week."

The Bishop of Byegumb has preached on Victory, I am certain,
(Though I haven't seen it mentioned in the Press).
But when I was his victim, how I wished I could have kicked
him,
For he made me love Religion less and less.

Published only in the *Cambridge Magazine*, 1 February 1919.

Devotion to Duty

I was near the King that day. I saw him snatch
And briskly scan the G.H.Q. dispatch.
Thick-voiced, he read it out. (His face was grave.)
"This officer advanced with the first wave,

And when our first objective had been gained,
(Though wounded twice), reorganized the line:
The spirit of the troops was by his fine
Example most effectively sustained."

He gripped his beard; then closed his eyes and said,
"Bathsheba must be warned that he is dead.
Send for her. I will be the first to tell
This wife how her heroic husband fell."

February 1919

Aftermath

Have you forgotten yet? . . .
For the world's events have rumbled on since those gagged days,
Like traffic checked while at the crossing of city-ways:
And the haunted gap in your mind has filled with thoughts that
        flow
Like clouds in the lit heaven of life; and you're a man reprieved
        to go,
Taking your peaceful share of Time, with joy to spare.
But the past is just the same—and War's a bloody game . . .
Have you forgotten yet? . . .
Look down, and swear by the slain of the War that you'll never forget.

Do you remember the dark months you held the sector at
        Mametz—
The nights you watched and wired and dug and piled sandbags
        on parapets?
Do you remember the rats; and the stench
Of corpses rotting in front of the front-line trench—
And dawn coming, dirty-white, and chill with a hopeless rain?
Do you ever stop and ask, "Is it all going to happen again?"

Do you remember that hour of din before the attack—
And the anger, the blind compassion that seized and shook you

As you peered at the doomed and haggard faces of your men?
Do you remember the stretcher-cases lurching back
With dying eyes and lolling heads—those ashen-grey
Masks of the lads who once were keen and kind and gay?

Have you forgotten yet? . . .
Look up, and swear by the green of the spring that you'll never forget.

March 1919

143

Everyone Sang

Everyone suddenly burst out singing;
And I was filled with such delight
As prisoned birds must find in freedom,
Winging wildly across the white
Orchards and dark-green fields; on——on——and out
      of sight.

Everyone's voice was suddenly lifted;
And beauty came like the setting sun:
My heart was shaken with tears; and horror
Drifted away . . . O, but Everyone
Was a bird; and the song was wordless; the singing will
      never be done.

April 1919

Atrocities

You told me, in your drunken-boasting mood,
How once you butchered prisoners. That was good!
I'm sure you felt no pity while they stood
Patient and cowed and scared, as prisoners should.

How did you do them in? Come, don't be shy:
You know I love to hear how Germans die,
Downstairs in dug-outs. "Camerad!" they cry;
Then squeal like stoats when bombs begin to fly.

      .   .   .

And you? I know your record. You went sick
When orders looked unwholesome: then, with trick
And lie, you wangled home. And here you are,
Still talking big and boozing in a bar.

Published in *War Poems*, October 1919.

Return of the Heroes

A lady watches from the crowd,
Enthusiastic, flushed, and proud.

"Oh! there's Sir Henry Dudster! Such a splendid leader!
How pleased he looks! What rows of ribbons on his tunic!
Such dignity . . . . Saluting. . . . *(Wave your flag now, Freda!)*. . . .
Yes, dear, I saw a Prussian General once—at Munich.

"Here's the next carriage! . . . Jack was once in Leggit's Corps
That's him! . . . I think the stout one is Sir Godfrey Stoomer.
They *must* feel sad to know they can't win any more
Great victories! . . . Aren't they glorious men? . . . so full of
    humour!"

Published in *War Poems*, October 1919.

A Footnote on the War

A Lenten blackbird singing in the square
Has called me to my window. Thence one sees
Sunshine—pale shadows cast by leafless trees—
And houses washed with light. One hears out there
A Sunday-morning patter of pacing feet,
And Time, in drone of traffic, drifting down the street.

When I was out in France, nine years ago,
The Front was doubly-damned with frost and snow:
Troops in the trenches cowered on the defensive,
While the smug Staff discussed the Spring Offensive.
Rest-camps, though regions where one wasn't killed,
Were otherwise disgusting: how we hated
Those huts behind Chipilly! Drafts we drilled
Were under-sized arrivals from belated
Chunks of the population, wrongly graded
As fit for active service. No one cursed
The weight of an equipment more than they did,
Poor souls! I almost think they were the worst
Soldiers who ever gulped battalion stew;
And how they fired their rifles no one knew.

We'd got a Doctor with a D.S.O.
And much unmedalled merit. In the Line
Or out of it, he'd taught the troops to know
That shells, bombs, bullets, gas, or even a mine
Heaving green earth toward heaven, were things he took
For granted, and dismissed with one shrewd look.
No missile, as it seemed, could cause him harm.

So on he went past endless sick-parades;
Jabbed his inoculation in an arm;
Gave "medicine and duty" to all shades
Of uninfectious ailment. Thus his name
Acquired a most intense, though local, fame.

Now here's his letter lying on my table,
Reminding me that, by some freak of chance,
He sauntered through three years of gory France
Unshot. And now, as amply as he's able,
He's quietly undertaken to compile
His late battalion's history. Every mile
They marched is safely stored inside his head . . .
I visualize the philosophic smile
That masks his wounding memories of the dead.

He asks me to contribute my small quota
Of reminiscence. What can I unbury? . . .
Seven years have crowded past me since I wrote a
Word on a war that left me far from merry.
And in those seven odd years I have erected
A barrier, that my soul might be protected
Against the invading ghosts of what I saw
In years when Murder wore the mask of Law.

Well—what's the contribution I can send?
Turn back and read what I've already penned
So jauntily. There's little left to say . . .
I'm not the man I was. Nine years have passed;
And though the legs that marched survive to-day,
My Fusiliering self has died away;
His active service came and went too fast.

He kept a diary. Reading what he wrote
Like some discreet executor I find

The scribbled entries moribund—remote
From the once-living context of his mind.
He wrote as one who craved to leave behind
A vivid picture of his personality
Foredoomed to swift extinction. He'd no craft
To snare the authentic moments of reality;
His mind was posing to be photographed;
"If I should die" . . . His notebook seldom laughed.

The distant Doctor asks me to report
That morning "when the Bosche attacked the Block",
When my detachment functioned to support
Some Cameronians who had "got the knock" . . .
Our own artillery fire was dropping short;
A sniper shot me through the neck; the shock
Is easy to remember. All the rest
Of what occurred that morning has gone west.

"The battle and the sunlight and the breeze;
Clouds blowing proud like banners;" lines like these
Were written in the way by many a poet
Whose words rang false, although he didn't know it.
The battle and the breeze were up that morning
For my detachment, stiff and chilled and yawning,
When out from underground they swore and stumbled;
The sun shone bright; intense bombardments grumbled,
And from their concrete-nests machine-guns rattled—
In fact the whole Brigade was properly embattled.

But how can I co-ordinate this room—
Music on piano, pictures, shelves of books,
And Sunday morning peace—with him for whom
Nine years ago the world wore such wild looks?
How can my brain join up with the plutonian
Cartoon? . . . The trench; and a fair-haired Cameronian

Propped in his pool of blood while we were throwing
Bombs at invisible Saxons . . . War's a mystery
Beyond my retrospection. And I'm going
Onward, away from that Battalion history
With all its expurgated dumps of dead:
And what remains to say I leave unsaid.

21–22 February 1926

Almost immediately S.S. relented and wrote a twelve-page account
(based on his diaries) of his experiences with the Second Battalion,
Royal Welch Fusiliers, in March–April 1917, which he sent to Dr J.C.
Dunn, DSO, MC (the doctor of the poem) for inclusion in Dunn's
anonymously compiled history of the battalion, *The War the Infantry
Knew 1914–1919*. This did not appear until 1938, by which time S.S.'s
contribution had long been incorporated in *Memoirs of an Infantry Officer*.
Text from manuscript.

To One Who was With Me in the War

It was too long ago—that Company which we served with . . .
We call it back in visual fragments, you and I,
Who seem, ourselves, like relics casually preserved with
Our mindfulness of old bombardments when the sky
With blundering din blinked cavernous.
                                    Yet a sense of power
Invades us when, recapturing an ungodly hour
Of ante-zero crisis, in one thought we've met
To stand in some redoubt of Time,—to share again
All but the actual wetness of the flare-lit rain,
All but the living presences who haunt us yet
With gloom-patrolling eyes.
                                    Remembering, we forget
Much that was monstrous, much that clogged our souls with
        clay
When hours were guides who led us by the longest way—
And when the worst had been endured could still disclose
Another worst to thwart us . . .
                                    We forget our fear . . .
And, while the uncouth Event begins to lour less near,
Discern the mad magnificence whose storm-light throws
Wild shadows on these after-thoughts that send your brain
Back beyond Peace, exploring sunken ruinous roads.
Your brain, with files of flitting forms hump-backed with loads,
On its own helmet hears the tinkling drops of rain,—
Follows to an end some night-relief, and strangely sees
The quiet no-man's-land of daybreak, jagg'd with trees
That loom like giant Germans . . .
                                    I'll go with you, then,
Since you must play this game of ghosts. At listening-posts
We'll peer across dim craters; joke with jaded men

Whose names we've long forgotten. (Stoop low there; it's the
    place
The sniper enfilades.) Round the next bay you'll meet
A drenched platoon-commander; chilled, he drums his feet
On squelching duck-boards; winds his wrist-watch; turns his
head,
And shows you how you looked,—your ten-years-vanished
    face,
Hoping the War will end next week . . .   .
                       What's that you said?

March 1926

On Passing the New Menin Gate

Who will remember, passing through this Gate,[1]
The unheroic Dead who fed the guns?
Who shall absolve the foulness of their fate,—
Those doomed, conscripted, unvictorious ones?
  Crudely renewed, the Salient holds its own.
  Paid are its dim defenders by this pomp;
  Paid, with a pile of peace-complacent stone,
  The armies who endured that sullen swamp.

Here was the world's worst wound. And here with pride
'Their name liveth for ever,' the Gateway claims.
Was ever an immolation so belied
As these intolerably nameless names?
Well might the Dead who struggled in the slime
Rise and deride this sepulchre of crime.

Begun Brussels, 25 July 1927; finished Campden Hill Square, January 1928

54,889 names are engraved on the gate.

War Experience

Degrees of groping thought have taught me to conclude
That when a man began in youth to learn truth crude
From life in the demented strife and ghastly glooms
Of soul-conscripting war-mechanic and volcanic,—
Not much remains, twelve winters later, of the hater
Of purgatorial pains. And somewhat softly booms
A Somme bombardment: almost unbelieved-in looms
The daybreak sentry staring over Kiel Trench crater.

Published in the *Spectator*, 2 June 1933.

Ex-Service

Derision from the dead
Mocks armamental madness.
Redeem (each Ruler said)
Mankind. Men died to do it.
And some with glorying gladness
Bore arms for earth and bled:
But most went glumly through it
Dumbly doomed to rue it.

The darkness of their dying
Grows one with War recorded;
Whose swindled ghosts are crying
From shell-holes in the past,
Our deeds with lies were lauded,
Our bones with wrongs rewarded.
Dream voices these—denying
Dud laurels to the last.

Published in the *Spectator*, 9 November 1934.

Asking for it

Lord God whose mercy guards the virgin jungle;
Lord God whose fields with dragon's teeth are farmed;
Lord God of blockheads, bombing-planes, and bungle,
Assist us to be adequately armed.

Lord God of cruelties incomprehensible
And randomized damnations indefensible,
Perfect in us thy tyrannous technique
For torturing the innocent and weak.

God of the dear old Mastodon's morasses
Whose love pervaded pre-diluvial mud,
Grant us the power to prove, by poison gases,
The needlessness of *shedding* human blood.

Published in *Time and Tide*, 10 November 1934.

Index of First Lines

157

He seemed so certain "all was going well", 89
He stood alone in some queer sunless place, 66
He stood in the gray trench and longed for home, 64
He turned to me with his kind, sleepy gaze, 25
He woke; the clank and racket of the train, 50
"He'd never seen so many dead before", 87
Here I'm sitting in the gloom, 36
He's got a Blighty wound. He's safe; and then, 101
His wet white face and miserable eyes, 41
Hullo! here's my platoon, the lot I had last year, 107

I am banished from the patient men who fight, 108
I found him in the guard-room at the Base, 86
I have come home unnoticed; they are still, 73
I keep such music in my brain, 62
I knew a simple soldier boy, 119
I lived my days apart, 60
I stood with the Dead, so forsaken and still, 123
I told her our Battalion'd got a knock, 81
I was near the King that day. I saw him snatch, 142
I watched a jostling mob that surged and yelled, 58
I'd been on duty from two till four, 28
I'd heard fool-heroes brag of where they'd been, 63
If, as I think, I'm warned to pack and go, 20
If I were fierce, and bald, and short of breath, 71
I'm back again from hell, 77
In fifty years, when peace outshines, 126
In red and gold the Corps-Commander stood, 65
It was too long ago——that Company which we served with, 151

"Jack fell as he'd have wished," the Mother said, 49

Lord God whose mercy guards the virgin jungle, 156
Lost in the swamp and welter of the pit, 118

Months and weeks and days go past, 122
Moonlight and dew-drenched blossom, and the scent, 111
Music of whispering trees, 39

Through darkness curves a spume of falling flares, 24
Time makes me be a soldier. But I know, 72
To these I turn, in these I trust, 29
Tossed on the glittering air they soar and skim, 99
Trudging by Corbie Ridge one winter's night, 55

We'd gained our first objective hours before, 105
Well, how are things in Heaven? I wish you'd say, 82
When I was young my heart and head were light, 117
When I'm among a blaze of lights, 67
When I'm asleep, dreaming and lulled and warm, 94
When life was a cobweb of stars for Beauty who came, 127
When roaring gloom surged inward and you cried, 44
When you are standing at your hero's grave, 136
Who will remember, passing through this Gate, 153
Why do you lie with your legs ungainly huddled, 129

You love us when we're heroes, home on leave, 100
You told me, in your drunken-boasting mood, 145
Young Croesus went to pay his call, 59
You've heard me, scornful, harsh, and discontented, 61